TRANSLATIONS OF CHRISTIAN LITERATURE
GENERAL EDITORS: W. J SPARROW-SIMPSON, D.D.
W. K. LOWTHER CLARKE, B.D.

SERIES I
GREEK TEXTS

THE DOCTRINE OF
THE TWELVE APOSTLES

THE DOCTRINE
OF THE
TWELVE APOSTLES

TRANSLATED INTO ENGLISH BY THE LATE
CHARLES BIGG, D.D.

WITH A NEW INTRODUCTION AND
REVISED NOTES BY
ARTHUR JOHN MACLEAN, D.D.
BISHOP OF MORAY, ROSS, AND CAITHNESS

WIPF & STOCK · Eugene, Oregon

Wipf and Stock Publishers
199 W 8th Ave, Suite 3
Eugene, OR 97401

The Doctrine of the Twelve Apostles
By Bigg, Charles and Maclean, Arthur John
Softcover ISBN-13: 978-1-6667-6331-7
Hardcover ISBN-13: 978-1-6667-6332-4
eBook ISBN-13: 978-1-6667-6333-1
Publication date 10/28/2022
Previously published by SPCK, 1922

This edition is a scanned facsimile of
the original edition published in 1922.

PREFACE TO THE NEW EDITION

To bring out a revised edition of Dr Bigg's *Doctrine of the Twelve Apostles* is not an easy task for one who, though he has learnt much from the writings of that eminent scholar, is unable to follow him in his argument in favour of a late date for this manual of instruction and worship. Dr Bigg took up an isolated position in assigning it to the fourth century; and as the present editor agrees with the great majority of those who have studied the question, in assigning it rather to the early part of the second century, it seems best to reproduce in the Introduction and Notes Dr Bigg's argument, as much as possible in his own words, and then to state, with all deference, the reasons why it does not appear to be conclusive. Since the first edition of this book was published, among the most important contributions to our knowledge of the subject are those by Dr J. Armitage Robinson and Dr C. H. Turner. These are considered in the Introduction and Notes, which also reproduce a very large part of Dr Bigg's discussions on the various points

PREFACE TO THE NEW EDITION

which have been raised. Many illustrations have been added from the series of Church Orders which have been made more fully known during the last twenty years, and in particular from the " so-called *Egyptian Church Order*," which has been shown by the investigations of Dom Connolly to date in the main from the time of Hippolytus himself. This discovery has thrown much light on the problem of the *Didache*.

INTRODUCTION

1. Scope of the Work.—The *Doctrine of the Twelve Apostles*, commonly known as the *Didache*, exists in a single manuscript, written A.D. 1056 by one "Leon, notary and sinner." It was first published in 1883 by Philotheus Bryennius, Metropolitan at that time of Serræ in Macedonia, and afterwards of Nicomedia, who had discovered the precious volume in 1873 in the library of the Jerusalem Monastery of the Most Holy Sepulchre at Constantinople. The manuscript is of great value because it contains, among other things, the only perfect Greek text of the Epistle of Clement of Rome to the Corinthians, and of the Ancient Homily formerly known as the Second Epistle of Clement. But for our present purpose the most important part of its contents is the *Didache*. When it was first discovered, this work was acclaimed as giving us a type of primitive Christianity, a picture of the religious condition of the whole Church in the age immediately succeeding that of the Apostles. Since that time there has been a considerable reaction, and the *Didache* has been described as a comparatively late and worthless romance, which tells us nothing of true history. In the following pages an endeavour will be made to show that neither of these views is in accordance with facts, but that, while the date is early, the work describes, not the conditions in the Church at large, but only those in a remote and backward district, where an imperfect Christianity was taught.

The **contents** of the *Didache* are as follows. (1) It begins with a Tract on the *Two Ways*, of Life and of Death, addressed, in the singular, to a catechumen in preparation for baptism, and to the Tract is added a short epilogue (i–vi). (2) Then follow ecclesiastical regulations and some prayers (vii–xv), the former addressed to the whole community, in the plural. (3) The book concludes with an apocalyptic chapter on the End of the world (xvi).

The whole book was, *c.* A.D. 375, incorporated, with additions and alterations suited to his own day, by the author of the *Apostolic Constitutions* (vii. 1–32).

2. The Tract on the Two Ways.—It is of the first importance for our subject to notice that this is an independent work (see on vi. 1, vii. 1), used in different ways by our author, in §§ 18–20 of the *Epistle of Barnabas*, and in §§ 4–13 of the "*Apostolic Church Order*," as we may call it, using the convenient name invented by Dr Bickell. Dr C. Taylor has, in his works on the *Didache*, given good reasons for believing that the *Two Ways* was originally a Jewish tract.

In Barnabas there is a great deal of it which is common to our work and the *Ap. Ch. Ord.*, but the sentences are arranged without any view to order. In the *Didache* and *Ap. Ch. Ord.*, on the other hand, (where the arrangement agrees, as far as they run in common,) the instruction is set forth in an orderly manner as a commentary on the Decalogue. Dr Salmon (*Dict. Chr. Biog.* iv. 811) remarks that Barnabas' want of order here resembles his mode of dealing with the Old Testament. Another point in considering the *Two Ways* is that there is a passage in the *Didache* (i. 3–6), based on the Sermon on the Mount, which is not found in the other two works, nor anywhere else before the *Apost. Const.;* this may probably be the work of the *Didache* writer himself.[1] It could not be part of the original *Two Ways*. The *Ap. Ch. Ord.* contains only the "Way of Life," and breaks off suddenly before the end of it. It must have been derived from a mutilated copy; see note on iv. 8. It must also be noticed that the chapters on the *Two Ways* are an integral part of Barnabas' Epistle. They are, indeed, omitted in the old Latin translation of that Epistle, but the translator ends with "habes interim de majestate Christi," etc., showing that what he had sent to his patron was an instalment only. Passages from §§ 18, 21

---

[1] Dr Robinson justly points out that the phrases "thou shalt be perfect" and "giveth according to the commandment" in i. 4 f. are repeated in vi. 2, xiii. 5, 7 (*Donnellan Lectures*, pp. 52, 55).

are quoted (as from Barnabas) by Clement of Alexandria (*Strom.* ii. 18 [84]) and Origen (*de Princ.* III ii. 4).

Thus we have to consider the relationship of Barnabas, *Ap. Ch. Ord.*, and the *Didache* with regard to the *Two Ways;* and before going further we may notice the dates which have been assigned to the first two books. Barnabas is dated A.D. 70–79 by Lightfoot (*Clement* ii. 505), A.D. 96–98 by Hilgenfeld, A.D. 119–138 by Harnack and Volkmar. The *Ap. Ch. Ord.* in its present form is usually dated *c*. A.D. 300, or a little earlier or a little later; but the part now in question exists separately in some MSS, and may be earlier than the rest of the book.

Now, with regard to the Tract, do any of these works borrow from another? The *Two Ways* in Barnabas and *Ap. Ch. Ord.* can hardly be derived from the *Didache;* for why should they have omitted the sections from the Sermon on the Mount? The *Didache* can hardly be derived from Barnabas, for we cannot conceive the writer picking out the precepts which occur in such a haphazard manner in Barnabas, and arranging them in order, as we have seen above; and moreover it is very unlikely that a borrower from Barnabas would have changed back his secondary "way of light" and "way of darkness" to the more original "way of life" and "way of death" (see on i. 1). The *Ap. Ch. Ord.* cannot be derived from Barnabas for the

§ 2] INTRODUCTION xi

same reasons; and further considerations which forbid this hypothesis are given in the notes on iii. 9, iv. 9. Again, it cannot be derived from the *Didache* for other reasons. The phrase about loving the preacher as the apple of the eye is both in it and in Barnabas but not in the *Didache* (see note on iv. 1); it must have been in the original *Two Ways*, and the *Ap. Ch. Ord.* did not get it from our present work. So with the phrase " and glorify him that redeemed thee from death" (see on *Did.* i. 2). Equally the *Didache* does not derive from the *Ap. Ch. Ord.*; see notes on iii. 2, 3, 9, where the former is certainly more original. Dr. Bigg, indeed, suggests that the phrase " my child " in *Didache* points to the fact that the copy from which it quotes had the sections divided among the apostles, as in *Ap. Ch. Ord.*[1] (see below, **3**), and that this points to the priority of the latter; but it is difficult to see the force of this argument. The conclusion, probably, is that all three writers quote independently from the *Two Ways*. It is exceedingly likely that many copies of that Tract, differing from each other, were in circulation. For possible connections between these writers in other parts of their works, see below, **5**.

But another question arises. Was the *Two Ways* in circulation in a Christian form before it

[1] In some cases with " my son " (or " my child "), usually in the same places as the *Didache*.

xii INTRODUCTION [§ 2

was used by these three writers? Apart from the Sermon on the Mount sections, which may have been the work of the *Didache* writer, there are New Testament quotations which are common to all three, or to two out of three; and these must therefore have been in the Tract as used by them. These are: Matt. v. 5 (*Did.* iii. 7, *q.v.*, and *Ap. Ch. Ord.* 11, not Barnabas); Acts iv. 32 (*Did.* iv. 8, Barn. 19—both have οὐκ ἐρεῖς ἴδια εἶναι—*Ap. Ch. Ord.* 13); Rom. xii. 9 (*Did.* v. 2, Barn. 20, both omitting the article, which is in Rom.—*Ap. Ch. Ord.* has not this chapter at all); Heb. xiii. 7 [1] (*Did.* iv. 1, *q.v.* [" God "], Barn. 19 [" Lord "], *Ap. Ch. Ord.* 12 [" God "]). Cf. also iv. 10, " the Spirit," as in Barn. 19 (*Ap. Ch. Ord.* wanting). Thus the answer to our question is probably in the affirmative. The Commandments in *Did.* ii. 3 give us no indication, as they would be independent of the Gospels.

Another view of the *Two Ways* is taken in the *Donnellan Lectures* for 1920 (below, § **10**), by Dr J. Armitage Robinson, who has kindly allowed the present editor to study advance proofs of that work, after this book was in type. Dr Robinson has departed from the view of the *Two Ways* which he held in 1912 when he

[1] This passage has μνημονεύετε, and speaks of departed teachers; the others have μνησθήσῃ, and speak of the living. It has been suggested that the phrase was a current Jewish one, and that the three writers, or their sources, are not quoting Hebrews.

wrote the article mentioned below in § 7, and now holds that it is not a Jewish tract Christianized, but was originally written as part of his Epistle by Barnabas, on whom the *Didache* writer and others depend for it. The Jewish tone of the tract Dr Robinson accounts for by the fact that Barnabas was Judaic in mind; the sudden change in Barn. 18, where the *Two Ways* is introduced, he accounts for by saying that Barnabas' style is disjointed and abrupt. He finds parallels to phrases of Barn. 18–20 in earlier chapters of that Epistle, such as " the knowledge that hath been given to us," " glorify him that redeemed thee from death," " bear malice against thy brother " (reminiscence of Zech. vii. 10; in Barn. 2 the similar Zech. viii. 17 is quoted), " love thy neighbour more than thine own soul," " from thy soul," and some others. This, he thinks, argues unity of authorship. Even, however, if there were no deduction to be made from this statement, the conclusion hardly follows, for there is no reason why Barnabas should not more than once have quoted or imitated phrases of a previously existing tract which appealed to him. But it is a curious fact that most of the phrases in question are not found in the *Didache* at all, and may possibly be Barnabas' own; and if so he may quite well have repeated them. A much more cogent argument is drawn (as it had been previously by Dr Harnack) from the fact that the precepts in the *Two Ways* are an "incongruous medley" in Barn., but are systematic in *Did.*; it is held that Barnabas could not have had the more systematic form before him, and deliberately have thrown it into such confusion (*Donn. Lect.*, p. 72). This is the opposite inference from that drawn above. Dr Salmon remarks (*Dict. Chr. Biog.* iv. 811) that the whole character of *Did.* makes us indisposed to think that its author was likely to have performed such a piece of literary workmanship as collecting the precepts scattered in Barn., digesting them into systematic order, and making to them a number of harmonious additions. Between these two views the reader must take his choice. There is, however, another consideration of great importance. To Dr Robinson's theory any proof of Barnabas being secondary to *Did.* is fatal, for according to that theory Barn. is the original; whereas a secondary phrase in *Did.* proves nothing on this head, if the *Two Ways* is anterior to both Barn. and *Did.* Barnabas, that is, may have preserved intact a phrase of the original which the *Didache* writer has altered; but that does not prove that the latter derives from the former. For example, Barnabas (§ 18) has two angels; *Did.* (i. 1) has not. If the omission is a sign of *Did.* being secondary, the only conclusion that can be drawn is that the original *Two Ways* had the angels, and that *Did.* for some reason omitted them; the omission is compatible with either

§ 2] INTRODUCTION xv

theory. So with other instances (see, *e. g.*, on *Did.* ii. 3). On the other hand it is difficult to follow Dr Robinson in holding that Barnabas' phrase about remembering the day of judgment (§ 19. 10 = *Did.* iv. 1, where see note) is not secondary; or that the Barnabas passages corresponding to *Did.* iv. 6, v. 2 are original; or that "the way of light and darkness" were altered in *Did.* to "the way of life and death," especially as Barnabas has retained "the way of death" in an incidental phrase (see on *Did.* i. 1). But this is fatal to Dr Robinson's theory. Further the change from the singular to the plural in *Did.* shows that our author used an older document which had the singular "my child" (see notes on v. 2, vii. 1); but this mode of address is not found in Barn., and the older document therefore was not that Epistle. Similar conclusions seem to follow from the phenomena of the *Ap. Ch. Ord.* mentioned above. The idea that that manual omitted some things of *Did.* (like i. 3-6) and added others under influence of Barnabas is much less likely than the view that many versions of the *Two Ways* were current, and that each writer was influenced by that which was best known to himself. See also note on *Did.* iv. 8; the "Way of Death (Darkness)" is in Barn. but not in *Ap. Ch. Ord.* Thus the latter writer can hardly have had Barnabas before him. For these reasons Dr Robinson's theory appears to be less probable. Undoubtedly as he remarks (p. 69), in a question like this allowance must be made for the subjective element; considerations which appeal to one mind do not appeal to another.[1]

The *Two Ways* was probably known to Lactantius (early fourth century), who seems to have taken the idea of his treatise on "the way of life and way of death" from it (*Div. Inst.* vi. 3 f., *Epitome* 59). Cf. also the *Testament of the Twelve Patriarchs* (second century?): "Two ways hath God given to the sons of men . . . there are two ways of good and evil" (*Asher*, § 1); but the idea is not much developed.

3. The Title.—This, with variations, is common to several works. The *Ap. Ch. Ord.*[2] has the following title in the *Syriac Octateuch*, where it is the third book, coming after the two books of the *Testament of our Lord :* "The third book of Clement, Teaching of the Twelve Apostles,"[3] and so in the subscription. This work, as we have seen, divides the sections between the apostles, of whom the writer had a curious list,

[1] In any case it may be said that Dr Robinson's view of the *Two Ways* has no very great bearing on his other theory, that mentioned below in § 7. It is quite possible to maintain the one without adhering to the other.

[2] See Dr. Arendzen's Syriac text with translation and notes in the *Journ. of Theol. Studies* iii. 60, the edition here chiefly used.

[3] Lagarde omits "Twelve," and adds: "in which those words are contained which each of the apostles spoke." In the Greek the title is: "The Constitutions (διαταγαί) through Clement, and Ecclesiastical Canons of the holy apostles."

§ 3] INTRODUCTION xvii

making Peter different from Cephas, naming Nathanael but not James the Less and Matthias. Thus we read: "John said, There are two ways . . ., Matthew said, Whatsoever things thou wouldest not . . ., Peter said, Thou shalt not kill . . .," and so on. A similar method was afterwards adopted in the eighth book of the *Apostolic Constitutions*, but not in the seventh book which incorporates the *Didache*.

Similarly Hippolytus (early third century) named one of his works *The Apostolic Tradition*, and Dom R. H. Connolly has shown that this has to a large extent survived in a Latin and some Oriental versions (*The So-called Egyptian Church Order and Derived Documents*, Cambridge, 1916). At the end of this Church Order [1] it is spoken of as the "tradition of the apostles" (Connolly, p. 194). Towards the end of the fourth century the writer of the *Apostolic Constitutions* prefixes to his complete work the title "Constitutions (διαταγαί) of the holy apostles through Clement," and begins it with: "The apostles and the presbyters to all among the Gentiles [cf. *Didache*] who believe on the Lord Jesus Christ." There is an Epitome of Book viii of *Apost. Const.* (or of an earlier draft of it), which used to be known as "Constitutions through Hippolytus," and which divides its matter into five sections thus: (1) "Didascalia

[1] It will be referred to as the *Eg. Ch. Ord.*, though it is probably not Egyptian but Roman in origin.

of the holy apostles about gifts;" (2) "Constitutions (διατάξεις) of the holy apostles about ordinations through Hippolytus;" (3) "Constitutions of the holy apostle Paul about ecclesiastical canons;" (4) "Constitutions of Peter and Paul the holy apostles;" (5) "Didascalia about good order, of all the holy apostles." Similarly the canons attached in many manuscripts to *Apost. Const.* viii are headed "Canons of the holy apostles"; some add "through Clement," with several variations (F. X. Funk, *Didascalia et Constitutiones Apostolorum*, Paderborn, 1905, i. 564). The *Older Didascalia* (third century), on which the first six books of *Apost. Const.* are based, is headed "Didascalia, that is, the catholic doctrine of the Twelve Apostles and holy disciples of our Saviour" (Funk, i. 2). The *Edessene Canons* (*c.* A.D. 350) are entitled "The Teaching of the apostles."

We have some references to a work or works with a similar title. Pseudo-Cyprian (*de Aleatoribus*, third century?) refers to the "Doctrina (or Doctrinae) Apostolorum." Eusebius (*H.E.* iii. 25, early fourth century) includes in his list of "spurious writings" (ἐν τοῖς νόθοις) the "so-called teachings of the apostles" (τῶν ἀποστόλων αἱ λεγόμεναι διδαχαί); Athanasius speaks (*Ep. Fest.* 39 [I. ii. 963 Ben.]) of a "so-called Teaching of the apostles" as useful for the instruction of catechumens. Rufinus, repeating Athanasius' statement in Latin, calls it

§ 4] INTRODUCTION xix

" Duae viae, vel Judicium secundum Petrum" (*Comm. in Symb. Apost.* 38, early fourth century; cf. Jerome, *de Vir. Ill.* 1). In the ninth century Nicephorus, patriarch of Constantinople, mentions " The Doctrine of the apostles," and says that it contained 200 lines (στίχοι); the line being the accurate trade measurement by which the copyists of manuscripts were paid and the price of books regulated, and consisting of 35 letters. This would refer to a shorter book than our *Didache*. On the whole, the title being so common, we cannot determine whether any of the above writers refer to our present work. On the meaning of the title see below, **7**.

4. General characteristics of the book. — The Jewish character of the instruction given is very striking, and there is hardly any interest shown in the history of our Lord's earthly life. There is very little grasp of the principles of the Incarnation, of the Atonement, of the Sacraments, or of the doctrine of the Holy Spirit,[1] though Trinitarian doctrine is implied by the baptismal formula (vii. 1), and though x. 6 may perhaps refer to our Lord as the God of David, and ix. 4 implies a doctrine of mediation. The writer is little influenced by St Paul or St John (see below, **5** *a*). Yet something must be deducted from this severe verdict when we remember that the *Two Ways* was not the original work of the author; its Jewish *provenance*, for example, will

[1] But see iv. 10, xi. 7-9, 12.

account for the negative form of the Golden Rule (i. 2). Whatever deductions we make, however, the legatistic tone is noticeable; baptism is merely an ordinance; the agape (or eucharist, if that is the subject of ix) is a Jewish meal Christianized, though the eucharist is recognized as the Christian sacrifice.

The doctrinal standpoint, then, is not that of the Church at large in any century. The author was probably a Jewish Christian much isolated from the thought of the Church as a whole. But he was entirely alienated from the non-Christian Jews. In many ways he shows this; he calls all the Jews " the hypocrites," whose fasts are to be avoided (viii. 1 f.); he does not advocate circumcision, and thus is a liberalized Jew; and he writes for a Gentile community (title).

There is no mention of women throughout the book. Sabatier deduces from this fact Jewish influence and early date (*La Didachè*, p. 153).

5. Relation of the Didache to other writings. —(*a*) *The New Testament*.—It is of great importance to ascertain how many books of the New Testament our writer knew, and what use he made of them. Before going into details, however, we must make some deductions when we remember the possibility of some features, like the Lord's prayer, the baptismal formula, Maranatha, Hosanna, and the biblical allusions

INTRODUCTION

in the prayers, having come to the author not direct from the Scriptures but through liturgical usage; also we must bear in mind that some of the New Testament references in the *Two Ways*, *i.e.* those outside i. 3–6, came to him indirectly (see above, **2**). On the other hand it has been suggested that the writer, wishing to pass himself off for a contemporary of the apostles (see below, **7**), veiled his New Testament allusions, as he was supposed to be writing at a time when much of it was not yet written; though to this it may be replied that he must have known that the First Gospel, which he quotes without the least disguise, was written long after St Paul's Epistles. There are clear references to St Matthew in i. 3–6, iii. 7, vii. 1, viii. 1, ix. 5, x. 5, xii. 1, xiii. 1, xvi. 1, 3–6, 8, where see notes; in several of these quotations there are references also to St Luke, whose special words and phrases are joined to those of the First Evangelist. Moreover, as the *Didache* writer certainly knew Acts (see below), it is probable that he also knew the Third Gospel. There is no evidence that he knew the Second. It is disputed whether he knew the Fourth (see notes on vii. 1, ix. 3 f., x. 1 f.); but Dr Turner justly remarks in his Note L (on the *Didache*), added to Dr Gore's *Church and the Ministry* (edition 1919), that there is no evidence of "intimate and conscious dependence"; the thought is incompatible with that of St John, and coincidences of language must not be pressed too far if the ideas are so different. With Acts our author was certainly acquainted; see the notes on vi. 2 f., viii. 2 f., ix. 2 f., x. 2 f., xiv. 1; the quotation in iv. 8 is not direct. Of the Epistles we can only affirm, and that not quite positively, that the writer knew 1 Corinthians; see notes on vi. 3, ix. 2, 4, x. 6, xi. 1. There may be references to the Thessalonian Epistles in xii. 3, xvi. 4 (that in iii. 1 is probably not direct), and to 1 Peter in i. 4, iv. 7, xvi. 5, possibly to 1 John in x. 5. Those to Hebrews and Romans in iv. 1, v. 2 are not direct. For the other New Testament books we have no evidence.

(b) *Barnabas*.—Apart from the *Two Ways*, there is a possible connection in *Did.* xvi. 26, where see notes. It is more probable that they are independent.

(c) *Hermas*.—This is a more difficult question; see note on i. 5 for the facts. There is an undoubted literary connection here. Dr Bigg thinks that the *Didache* writer is quoting and combining Hermas and the apocryphon found in Clement of Alexandria—he believes the apocryphon to be Clement's own—and is therefore later than both those writers. Dr Harnack, on the other hand, in his *Chronologie der Altchr. Lit.* (Leipzig, 1897), thinks that the apocryphon is the source of the passages in Hermas and the *Didache*. However this may be, we notice that the phrase " Woe to him that receiveth " is all

§ 5] INTRODUCTION xxiii

that our writer has in common with the apocryphon, and that is not very close; all that Hermas has in common with it is " receive in hypocrisy " which is not in the *Didache*. Thus it might equally be said that Hermas was combining the *Didache* with the apocryphon. We have no means of determining the date of the latter; it may well be an old Jewish saying, and we can put Clement here out of the question. We have, then, to ask whether the *Didache* is quoting Hermas, or Hermas the *Didache*. Either supposition is possible, but the phrase " he is guiltless," which occurs once in Hermas, twice in the *Didache*, has more sense in the latter; indeed we can hardly explain the former without reading the latter. Our author says that he who receives because he is in need is guiltless, just as he had said that the giver is guiltless; but Hermas says only that " he that giveth is guiltless." Who could doubt it, and why should it be said? But as part of the larger saying it is intelligible. It seems probable therefore (though this is much disputed [1]) that the *Didache* here has the priority. But what is the date of Hermas? Here again there is much difference of opinion. Internal and external evidence contradict each other. Hermas himself mentions " Clement," who can hardly be other than Clement of Rome (*c.* A.D. 95), as a contemporary; but the *Muratorian Fragment* (*c.* A.D. 200?) says that he wrote while his

[1] See Robinson, *Donn. Lect.*, p. 53 f.

brother Pius occupied the Roman see, *i. e.* in the middle of the second century, if indeed it be the case that the Greek original of the *Fragment* (now lost) said that Hermas wrote *during the episcopate* of Pius. On these facts two dates have been chosen for Hermas : either A.D. 140–155 (Lightfoot, and the majority of scholars), or at the very beginning of that century (Salmon, *Dict. Chr. Biog.* ii. 912, Caspari, Zahn).

(*d*) *Clement of Alexandria* quotes the saying given in *Did.* iii. 5, probably as " Scripture." He therefore either quotes our author, which is probable, or some form of the *Two Ways* older than himself. It is not probable that our writer is here quoting Clement, for his copy of the *Two Ways* must have had this saying in it if, as is urged above, the *Ap. Ch. Ord.* writer (who also has it) knew that Tract independently of the *Didache*. The parallel to Clement in *Did.* ix. 2 (" vine of David ") is probably not a quotation on either side, certainly not on the side of our author; see note there. The same may be said of *Did.* ix. 3.

(*e*) *Origen.*—There is a possible connection in *Did.* iii. 10, *q.v.*; Origen is professedly quoting, but probably from Barnabas. The connection in *Did.* ix. 2 is unlikely.

(*f*) *The Apostolic Church Order.*—For the *Two Ways*, see above, **2**. The only other connection is commented on at *Did.* x. 3, where the priority of *Ap. Ch. Ord.* is impossible.

§ 5] INTRODUCTION xxv

(*g*) *The " Egyptian Church Order."*—The points of contact are " gathering together into one " (*Did.* ix. 4) and the cup at the agape (ix. 2). But this need mean no literary connection. The conditions described in the *Didache* are far less developed than those in the " *Eg. Ch. Ord.*," whatever cause we may assign to the fact (below, **7**); for example, the doxologies to the prayers are much shorter in our author (see on ix. 2).

(*h*) *Tatian.*—Dr Bigg thinks that our writer must have used Tatian's *Diatessaron* because both weave together in much the same way parallel verses in the First and Third Gospels (*Did.* i. 3-6, xvi. 1), and because Tatian is said by Theodoret to have suppressed the title " Son of David " for our Lord (see note on *Did.* x. 6). But Tatian was not the only " harmonizer." Justin's gospel quotations greatly resemble in character those of the *Didache, e. g. Apol.* i. 34, where he combines Luke i. 31 f. and Matt. i. 21, as if both sayings were addressed to St Mary.

(*i*) *The Older Didascalia* (third century).—Dr Bigg thinks that *Did.* i. 3 (*q.v.*) : " fast for them which persecute you " is derived from *Didasc.* v. 13 f. (Funk i. 268 ff.). But it is difficult to see why the short saying of *Didache* should be derived from the long injunction of *Didascalia*. Dr Bigg thinks that the words of *Didascalia* imply " not only the Lenten fast but the Quartodeciman controversy," and that the *Didache*, being later than *Didascalia*, took the side of the opponents of the Quartodecimans. Is not all this a begging of the question? Our author does not mention Lent or Easter at all. The idea of fasting on behalf of others may be Jewish, but he was a Jewish Christian.

(*j*) *Sarapion of Thmuis and* [*Pseudo-*]*Athanasius de Virginitate* (fourth century).—See on ix. 4. Here undoubtedly we have quotations from the *Didache*.

6. Date of the Didache.—When the *Didache* was first published, it was generally agreed that it was a very early work, probably of the beginning of the second century, though some placed it in the first, others (who judged that it quotes Hermas) in the middle of the second. In 1898 Dr Bigg proposed the theory that it was a romance of the fourth century, and he truly remarked that the date must be ascertained in the usual manner, by a rigorous application of the usual tests. He urged that it will be fixed not by any historical theory, certainly not by a historical theory largely based upon the book itself, but by the latest feature to which we are able, by help of external knowledge, to assign a definite or approximate time value. Accordingly he considered first the external evidence, and came to the conclusion that the *Didache* probably quotes, or is later than, Barnabas, Hermas, Tatian's *Diatessaron*, Cyprian (see below),

§ 6] INTRODUCTION xxvii

the *Apostolic Church Order*, and the *Older Didascalia*, and that Clement of Alexandria does not, as is usually thought, quote the *Didache*. Reasons have been urged in the preceding section of this Introduction, and in the Notes there referred to, for a contrary opinion. It seems probable that the only extant works that our author can be proved to have known are the Septuagint, certain books of the New Testament and a Christianized form of the *Two Ways*. The case of Hermas is doubtful, but it is suggested that the evidence points to our writer's independence of, or priority to, all the other works named.

Dr Bigg's argument for a later date from the internal evidence is here given, in his own words, in the left-hand column, while in the right-hand column reasons are given for thinking that they do not carry conviction, and that, in Dr Turner's words, the argument is " a paradox and nothing more."

1. Idolatry described, as in the Apologists, as the service of "dead gods" (vi. 3).	1. Why is this an indication of late date? In the second century Pseudo-Clement of Rome ("An Ancient Homily") and Melito use the phrase.
2. The clause in the Lord's prayer, understood as meaning not " deliver us from the Evil One " but " deliver us from evil " (viii. 2).	2. Why does this, if true, show a late date? Many moderns think that this was the First Evangelist's own interpretation.
3. The repeated phrase " the gospel " (or " his gospel " ; viii. 2, xi. 3, xv. 3 f.).	3. See note on viii. 2; the intermediate use of the word " gospel " rather favours an early date.

4. The phrase "confess in church" (iv. 14).	4. Why is this an indication of late date? The "church" is the Christian assembly, not the building (see note).
5. The three hours of prayer (viii. 3), and the fixed Wednesday and Friday fasts (viii. 1).	5. The three hours of prayer, if they are referred to, are a sign rather of early date (see note). The Wednesday and Friday fasts are found in the second century in Tertullian and Clement of Alexandria.
6. The eucharistic use of the text, "Give not that which is holy to the dogs" (ix. 5).	6. See note, and the parallels in Tertullian, Clement of Alexandria, and Hippolytus ("*Eg. Ch. Ord.*").
7. The singular way in which the agape is mentioned (xi. 9).	7. It is hard to see why this is an indication of late date.
8. The stress laid upon the persecution of Christians by Christians (xvi. 4). 9. The absence of all reference to persecution of Christians by heathen.	8, 9. The opposition of so-called Christians was a feature of Church life from the beginning, and the *Didache* is here merely quoting the First Gospel; the absence of mention of heathen persecutions does, indeed, point to a time of peace, but of these there were many in early times. Nothing is more remarkable in the external history of the Early Church than the partial nature of persecution by the heathen, especially before the middle of the third century.
10. The absence of chiliasm (xvi. 7).	10. Though some early fathers were Chiliasts or Millenarians, such as Irenæus and Papias, there seems to have been much difference

	of opinion on the subject in the second and third centuries, and there were many non-Chiliasts (see, *e. g.* Lightfoot, *Clement*, ii. 387). Our author does not condemn chiliasm, as he would probably do if he were a later writer who was a non-Chiliast; he only does not mention the subject when speaking of the Second Advent.
11. The absence of all interest in the humanity of our Lord (xvi. 6).	11. There is no reason why this should be a sign of a late, rather than of an early, date. It is equally true to say that the author shows little interest in the divinity of our Lord.
12. The traces of Alexandrine thought in the prayers.	12. The reference is apparently to the phrases " vine of David " and " life and knowledge " in ix. 2, 3, which are thought to show the influence of Clement of Alexandria and Origen. Reasons are given in the notes for thinking that our author cannot be quoting either. Certainly Sarapion and the *De Virginitate* quote a *Didache* prayer, but this fact tells us nothing about the date of the latter. It is also not certain that these prayers were the composition of our author.
13. Baptism by affusion (vii. 3). " It affords the most precise and conclusive time-indication of all."	13. This argument would prove the *Didache* to be later than Cyprian. But it appears to be based on a

	mistake. The two writers are speaking of totally different things (see note.)
14. The publication of the Lord's prayer and a collection of eucharistic prayers in a book of this description (viii. 2, ix. 2, 3, x. 1–5).	14. The "disciplina arcani" was no regular institution, and was as much in force (in so far as it was in force at all) at a later date as at an early one. In any case the Lord's prayer could be obtained at any time by the heathen by procuring a copy of the First or the Third Gospel. If Clement of Rome publishes a prayer (*Cor.* 59 ff.), why should not our author do the same thing?
15. The word "Christmonger" (χριστέμπορος, xii. 5). "It is so used as to form an epigram—'Not Christians but Christmongers.' . . . The epigram was, in fact, a current fourth-century byword, and dates the book in which it is found as certainly as the 'tragedy' of the Pseudo-Phalaris."	15. This argument, and that about baptism by affusion, appear to be those on which Dr Bigg chiefly relied. Dr Turner (*op. cit.*, p. 374 *n.*) remarks that some one must have invented the word χριστέμπορος; why not a writer in the second century, if Ignatius could coin χριστόνομος, χριστοφόρος, χριστομαθία (Ignat. *Rom.* inscr., *Eph.* 1, *Philad.* 8)? This argument of Dr Bigg is similar to that urged against the authenticity of the Ignatian Epistles because of the use of the word "leopard"; see Lightfoot, *Ignatius and Polycarp* ii. 212 (*Rom.* 5).

For the reasons stated, then, it must be held that the argument for a fourth-century date have

§ 7]   INTRODUCTION   xxxi

failed. We will consider further arguments for an early date in the sequel.

7. Does the Didache give a true picture of Christian life?—Another attack was made on the usually accepted view as to the date of this work by Dr J. Armitage Robinson, Dean of Wells, in his essay on "The Problem of the Didache" in the *Journal of Theological Studies* xiii. 339 (1912).[1] He does not agree with Dr Bigg in assigning the book to the fourth century, and, while not fixing the date, thinks that it must have been written before the spread of Montanism. But he raises a question which has a great bearing on the date. He maintains that the picture of life painted by our author is a purely imaginary one, and that there never was a community of Christians whose circumstances were those of this work. The writer, he thinks, was well versed in his New Testament, and constructed out of it what he thought, however erroneously, to be a true picture of Christian life in the first century, though this picture had no relation to the life of his own time; he is careful to veil his New Testament quotations,

---

[1] Reprinted as an appendix to his *Donnellan Lectures*, 1920. His contribution (on the Primitive Ministry) to Dr Swete's *Essays* (below, § 10) expressly refrains from discussing the question here considered; he combats in detail Dr Harnack's theory (deduced from the *Didache*) of a "charismatic" ministry of apostles, prophets and teachers, and a local "non-charismatic" ministry of bishops and deacons.

so as not to betray himself. Much the same line is taken by Mr G. Edmundson in his *Bampton Lectures* for 1913; and by Dr H. J. Wotherspoon in his *Ministry in the Church*—the latter is certain that the *Didache* cannot be earlier than the end of the second century, and that there is in it no primitive atmosphere, no charismatic enthusiasm, but a legalistic tone and a professional prophetism.

On the use of the New Testament by our author, see above, **5**. Dr Robinson has gone very thoroughly into this question, and in particular has urged the obligations of the *Didache* to 1 Corinthians. But he seems greatly to have overstated the references to the New Testament, and also, as Dr Turner remarks, we must not underrate the amount of Old Testament, Jewish, or Jewish-Christian liturgical language which would be at the disposal of any Christian writer at the beginning of the second century.

The gist of Dr Robinson's indictment, however, lies in the supposition that the author was a cunning forger who was desperately anxious to pass off his work as an apostolic writing published long before his day. We have therefore to consider the whole question of the **apostolic setting** of this and other works of the first five centuries. The present book is called " The Doctrine of the Twelve Apostles." [1] The fiction, if any, is found

---

[1] It is quite probable that this was the title of the Christianized *Two Ways* used by our author (above, **2**), and was not original with him.

§ 7]   INTRODUCTION   xxxiii

only in the title; it never appears again, as it does, for example, throughout the *Apostolic Church Order*, the *Older Didascalia* and its successors, the *Apostolic Constitutions*—which introduces it into vii. 2, 11, 22, though it is absent from the parallel sections of the *Didache*—and, in an aggravated form, throughout the *Testament of our Lord*, which professes to give the words of Jesus spoken to the disciples in the Great Forty Days. On the other hand the *Apostolic Tradition*[1] of Hippolytus, mentioned on the Chair in the Lateran Museum at Rome, has the fiction, if at all, only in the title and subscription (Connolly, p. 194), just as in the *Canons of Hippolytus* (a work probably of the fourth century or later) the only reference to the Hippolytean fiction is in the title.

In this connection we have to bear in mind that the habit of ascribing books to older writers was an extraordinarily common one, both among Jews and Christians.[2] Instances occur in the canonical books of the Bible, as in Ecclesiastes, where by a dramatic fiction Solomon is made to speak, in Deuteronomy, and perhaps in 2 Peter; in the Apocrypha, as in the Wisdom of Solomon; in the Jewish and Christian apocalyptic literature, as in the different books of

[1] Cf. Eusebius, *H.E.* iv. 8: Hegesippus records in five books the true tradition of apostolic doctrine (τὴν ἀπλανῆ παράδοσιν τοῦ ἀποστολικοῦ κηρύγματος).

[2] See the present editor's *Ancient Church Orders*, Cambridge, 1910, p. 5.

Enoch, and in the *Testament of the Twelve Patriarchs ;* among the Gnostic sects, as in the *Clementine Recognitions* and *Homilies.* What could be the meaning of all this ? Are we to regard this habit as a gigantic system of forgery? Or are we to look on it simply as the fashion of the time ? We may remember that we still retain the habit whenever we speak of the " Apostles' Creed " or the " Athanasian Creed." All we mean now by those phrases is that these creeds represent the doctrines of the apostles [1] and of Athanasius. And it is not too much to say the same thing of those who, like our author or Hippolytus, gave titles to their works which would denote that they taught what the apostles taught. If, with Dr Robinson, we regard the *Didache* writer as a crafty forger who uses all manner of questionable devices to cover up his deceit, we must say the same thing of Hippolytus and many others, even if we put aside for the sake of argument writers like the author of the *Apostolic Church Order*, who carry the " apostolic fiction " much further.

Moreover, we may ask what would be the use of all this supposed system of forgery? By their very nature most, if not all, of the Church Orders were intended for the use of the people themselves. But they would be useless if they

[1] This was the original meaning of the name " Apostles' Creed." The fiction that each clause was contributed by an individual apostle was of later growth. See C. H. Turner in Swete's *Essays*, p. 101.

were so full of antiquarianisms, or sham antiquarianisms, that they could not be recognized by their readers as suitable for their own age. It may be added that the disguise, even where the "fiction" is developed, is in many cases very thin, and that it was not likely that many would be deceived. Dr Robinson's theory not only postulates a scholar of no mean attainments, say at the end, or in the middle, of the second century, who could make up a romance out of his reading of the New Testament—and we may doubt if such a scholar then existed— but also that he gathered his materials not from observation of the life of his own community, but from the sacred records. Yet much of his work he could not have got from the New Testament. Whence then did he get it? And can we conceive a Christian writer at the end of the second century not knowing the whole, or almost the whole, of the New Testament? But, if so, why does he show practically no dependence on either Johannine or Pauline theology?

For these reasons it is not possible to subscribe to this theory. It is much more likely that the *Didache* represents a real state of things, but in a remote area; it exhibits, probably, a community of Christians hardly influenced by the writings of St Paul (except one Epistle) or of St John, but much influenced by the First Gospel; a community with a very meagre conception of the deepest truths of Christianity.

8. Conclusions from internal evidence of date.—If the *Didache* represents a real state of things, we must look for a time when the ministry embraced itinerant and local elements in combination; when the local ministers were styled "bishops" and "deacons," the former name being used in its New Testament sense; and when a supervision by non-local itinerants, called "apostles," "prophets" and "teachers"—these names probably all representing one class (see on xi. 1)—was a part of the Church constitution. But this could only be when the system of diocesan episcopacy had not yet been everywhere established (see note on xv. 1). There are signs in the *Didache* that the position of itinerants was still a strong one. The "prophets" are very prominent. On the other hand, they are not in the least like those of Montanism, and there are no prophetesses as in that system (see on xi. 7). After the middle of the second century the genuine prophet in catholic communities only just survived. This all points to a date early in the century. Dr Turner concludes for *c.* A.D. 100; but the question of the dependence of the *Didache* on Hermas, and the date of Hermas, remain doubtful, and we may have therefore to put our book somewhat later. From internal evidence alone we should put it at the very beginning of the century.

Dr Sabatier places the *Didache c.* A.D. 50, before St Paul's Epistles were written or known.

§ 10] INTRODUCTION xxxvii

But this is very unlikely; 1 Corinthians was most probably known to our author, and his ignorance of Pauline theology was more probably due to remoteness of country rather than to priority of time.

9. Place of writing.—On this point there are few indications; Egypt is apparently the country where the *Didache* (apart from the *Two Ways*) is first quoted (see on ix. 4), but the mention of " mountains " in that passage makes Egypt unlikely. Our book is incorporated in part of the *Apostolic Constitutions*, a Syrian work, and therefore Syria is a possible home of the author. Dr Taylor (*Teaching*, p. 116) prefers North Palestine. A slight argument for Syria might be deduced from the fact that the doxology to the Lord's prayer, for which the *Didache* is perhaps the oldest authority, is said to have originated in liturgical use in Syria (Westcott-Hort, *Notes on Select Readings*, p. 9); also from the extended use of the word " apostle " (see on xi. 3). But the indications are so slight that it would be venturesome to come to a definite conclusion on this subject.

10. Bibliography.—The following works, among others, will be found useful for a study of the subject.

A. HILGENFELD, *Novum Testamentum extra canonem receptum*, fasc. iv. (ed. 2), Leipzig, 1884.

A. HARNACK, *Die Lehre der zwölf Apostel*, in " Texte und Untersuchungen " ii. 1, Leipzig, 1884. Contains also *Ap. Ch. Ord.* and *Apost. Const.* vii. 1–32.

xxxviii INTRODUCTION

T. ZAHN, *Forschungen zur Geschichte des N.T.-lichen Kanons und der altkirchl. Lit.*, part iii, p. 278, Erlangen, 1884.

P. SCHAFF, *The Oldest Church Manual*, 1885.

R. D. HITCHCOCK and F. BROWN, *The Teaching of the Twelve Apostles*, new ed., London, 1885. Contains a very full Bibliography up to 1885.

H. D. M. SPENCE, *The Teaching of the Twelve Apostles*, London, 1885.

P. SABATIER, *La Didachè*, ed. 2, Paris, 1885.

C. TAYLOR, *Teaching of the Twelve Apostles*, Cambridge, 1886; *Essay on the Theology of the Didache*, with Greek text, Cambridge, 1889.

G. SALMON, article "Teaching of the Twelve Apostles," in Smith-Wace's *Dictionary of Christian Biography*, London, 1887, iv. 806; discussion in his *Historical Introduction to the New Testament*, ed. 6, London, 1892, xxvi.

J. B. LIGHTFOOT and J. R. HARMER, *Apostolic Fathers*, London, 1891. Greek texts and translations.

L. E. ISELIN, *Eine bisher unbekannte Version des ersten Theiles der "Apostellehre,"* in "T. und Unt." xiii. 1, Leipzig, 1895. Contains a short Oriental version of the *Two Ways*.

J. SCHLECHT, *Doctrina* xii *Apostolorum*, Freiburg in Br., 1900. Contains the complete Latin version of the *Two Ways*.

J. WORDSWORTH, *The Ministry of Grace*, London, 1901.

J. ARMITAGE ROBINSON, article "The Problem of the Didache" in the *Journal of Theological Studies*, London, 1912, xiii. 339; *Barnabas, Hermas, and the Didache* (Donnellan Lectures), London, 1920.

C. GORE and C. H. TURNER, *The Church and the Ministry*, new ed., London, 1919, Note L, p. 367. This elaborate note is now brought up to date.

H. B. SWETE, *Essays on the Early History of the Church and the Ministry*, by various writers, London, 1918.

The Greek Text of the *Didache* is published by S.P.C.K., London, 1920, price 4*d*. (Texts for Students No. 13.) An English Translation (No. 13a), without notes, price 3*d*.

DOCTRINE OF THE TWELVE APOSTLES

DOCTRINE OF THE LORD THROUGH THE TWELVE APOSTLES TO THE GENTILES

CHAPTER I

1. There are two Ways, one of Life and one of Death, and there is much difference between the

Titles.—The book has two titles, a longer and a shorter; for similar titles in other works see Introduction, § 3. They are founded on Acts ii. 42 (τῇ διδαχῇ τῶν ἀποστόλων), and the phrase here "to the Gentiles (ἔθνεσιν)" may come from Matt. xxviii. 19 "make disciples of all the nations (ἔθνη)." Dr Salmon suggests (*Intr. to N.T.*, p. 560) that the original *Two Ways* was a manual of instruction for Gentile proselytes to Judaism; if so the phrase may not come from the First Gospel. Even if it was not original in our author, he would hardly have used it unless he was a Jewish Christian.

The tract on the Two Ways.—The Way of Life.—See Introd., § 2, for the use of this tract by Barnabas and the *Apostolic Church Order* writer and other authorities. The *Ap. Ch. Ord.* has (unlike Barnabas) much the same order as the *Didache* in the tract, but is more diffuse, and adds sentences.

I. 1. *Ways . . . of Life and . . . Death.* The idea is from Jer. xxi. 8; cf. Deut. xxx. 15, 19, Prov. xii. 28, Ecclus. xv. 17, Matt. vii. 13 f. We may compare the name "the Way"

two Ways. 2. The Way then of Life is this : Firstly, thou shalt love God who made thee :

for Christianity in Acts ix. 2, etc. Barnabas has altered " life " and " death," which are clearly original, to "light " and " darkness " (§ 18), though he has, perhaps by inadvertence, retained the words " way of death " in an incidental sentence of § 19. After saying that there is a great difference between the two ways, he adds that over the one way are set (τεταγμένοι) light-giving angels of God, over the other angels of Satan. A similar phrase is found in the Latin version of the *Two Ways*.

2. *who made thee.* Both Barnabas and *Ap. Ch. Ord.* add, "and glorify him that redeemed thee from death." Thus the latter work cannot have been dependent on the *Didache* alone (Introd., § 2).

do not. The negative form of the Golden Rule (Matt. vii. 12, Luke vi. 31); cf. Tob. iv. 15 " what thou thyself hatest do to no man," quoted by Clement of Alexandria (*Strom.* ii. 23). It is also found, not quite in the words of the *Didache*, in Codex Bezae (D) and some cursives at Acts xv. 20, 29; and in some Fathers, *e. g.* Theophilus of Antioch (second century) : " Whatever a man would not wish to be done to himself, he should not do to another" (*ad Autol.* ii. 34), and Tertullian (*adv. Marc.* iv. 16), who says that the negative form is implied in the positive. It is also found in *Ap. Ch. Ord.*, nearly in the words of Tobit; but not in either form in Barnabas.

Interpolation from the Sermon on the Mount.—3-6. These sections are based on Matt. v. 44, 46, 39-42, Luke vi. 27-30, 32-35, woven together. Neither evangelist's order is quite accurately preserved, and the language is paraphrased. Our writer keeps some of the words peculiar to the First Gospel, *e. g.* " them that persecute you," " Gentiles " (Luke " sinners "), " a blow " ῥάπισμα (Matt. ῥαπίζει), " turn to him the other also," " if any compel . . . two "; and some of those peculiar to the Third, *e. g.* " bless them which curse you " (not in the best text of Matt.), " what thank," " love " (present tense), " give " δίδου (Matt. δός), " ask not again," " what is thine " τὸ σόν (Luke τὰ σά, not in Matt.). See Introd., § 5.

THE DIDACHE

secondly, thou shalt love thy neighbour as thyself: and whatsoever thou wouldest not have done to thyself, do not thou either to another. 3. Now the doctrine of these words is this : Bless them which curse you, and pray for your enemies, and fast for them which persecute you. For what thank have ye, if ye love them which love you? Do not even the Gentiles the same? But do ye love them which hate you, and ye shall have no enemy. 4. Abstain from fleshly and bodily lusts. If any one give thee a blow on the right cheek, turn to him the other also, and thou shalt be perfect. If any compel thee to go one mile, go

3. *the doctrine . . . is this.* This phrase was also in the *Two Ways* as used by *Ap. Ch. Ord.*, which has "The doctrine of these words speak thou (Sah, give thou to them) O our (my) brother Peter" (§ 5). Then follows : " Peter said, Thou shalt not kill," etc. (§ 6).

for your enemies and fast. Interpolated into the Matthean saying, "pray for them that persecute you " (best text), which, however, has " Love your enemies." There is a parallel to " fast for them which persecute you " in the *Older Didascalia* (third century) : " When ye fast, pray and make request for them that are perishing, as we also [the apostles] did when our Saviour suffered " (v. 13, Funk, *Didasc. et Const. Ap.* i. 268). After a long interval we read : " For the sake of your brethren ye did this [fasting on Wednesday and Friday]. . . . But again also on Friday (*parasceve*) fast for them because they crucified me. . . . Pray for your enemies. As to our fast in Pascha, ye shall fast because of the disobedience of our brethren. . . . For them . . . we ought to fast and mourn " (v. 14, Funk, i. 276, 280; see Introd., § 5). This is said also, more shortly, in *Apost. Const.* v. 14.

4. *Abstain*, perhaps an expansion of 1 Pet. ii. 11. For " bodily " (σωματικῶν) some editors needlessly read "worldly" (κοσμικῶν) as *Ap. Const.* vii. 2.

with him two : if any take thy cloak, give him also thy tunic : if any take from thee what is thine, ask for it not again : for indeed thou canst not. 5. Give to every one that asketh thee, and ask it not again; for the Father willeth that we should give to all from his own gifts. Blessed is he that giveth according to the commandment : for he is guiltless : woe to him that receiveth : for if one receiveth because he hath need, he shall be guiltless : but he that hath no need shall render account why he received and

5. Here is the one literary connection between the *Didache* and Hermas. The latter in *Mand.* ii. 4–6 says : " Give to all that are in want freely, not doubting (διστάζων ; so *Did.* iv. 7, *Ap. Ch. Ord.* 13, Barn. 19) to whom thou shalt give and to whom thou shalt not give. Give to all, for to all God willeth that there should be given (δίδοσθαι θέλει, so *Did.* θ. δ.) of his own bounties (δωρημάτων ; *Did.* " gifts," χαρισμάτων). They, then, that receive shall render an account to God why they received it, and to what end ; for they that receive in distress shall not be judged, but they that receive in hypocrisy shall pay the penalty. He, then, that giveth is guiltless " (ἀθῷος, so *Did.*). Also an apocryphon found in Clement of Alexandria (A. Resch, *Agrapha*, " T. und Unt.," Leipzig, 1889, p. 99) has : " Woe to them that have and receive in hypocrisy, or are able to help themselves and yet receive from others. For he that hath and receiveth through hypocrisy or idleness shall be condemned." This apocryphon is almost exactly quoted in the *Older Didascalia* and in *Ap. Const.* iv. 3 (Funk, i. 220 f.) and for this reason the words of *Did.*, " Woe to him that receiveth," etc., are omitted in the parallel *Ap. Const.* vii. 7. For the relation of Hermas and the *Didache* see Introd., § 5. Hermas has the *idea* of the " two ways " (straight and crooked) in *Mand.* vi. 1.

Blessed . . . commandment, perhaps referring to Acts xx. 35.

shall not . . . farthing, from Matt. v. 26, very closely.

THE DIDACHE

for what, and being cast into straits shall be examined concerning what he did, and shall not come out thence till he have paid the uttermost farthing. 6. But about this it hath also been said: Let thine alms sweat into thy hands, until thou know to whom thou art to give.

CHAPTER II

1. And the second commandment of the doctrine is this: 2. Thou shalt not kill, thou shalt not commit adultery, thou shalt not corrupt boys, thou shalt not commit fornication, thou shalt not steal, thou shalt not use magic, thou shalt not practise sorcery, thou shalt not procure abortion, nor kill the new-born child. Thou shalt not covet thy neighbour's goods. 3. Thou

6. The source of this quotation is unknown. Cassiodorus (fifth century) has the same phrase with "find a just man" for "know" (Resch, *Agrapha*, p. 288). The meaning seems to be "Work hard to make money which you can give to the needy when the occasion arises."

II. 1. We now return to the original *Two Ways*, and Barnabas and *Ap. Ch. Ord.* run on parallel lines, the former with much diversity of order. The introductory words are peculiar to the *Didache*. What follows is an exposition of the "second commandment," Thou shalt love thy neighbour as thyself.

2, 3. For this form of the Commandments cf. the addition in Mark x. 19, "Defraud not," and the variations in order in the other Synoptists. The order in Exod. xx. 12 is not the same as that in Deut. v. 16 LXX, and in both the order differs from that in the Gospels. In Mark and Luke we have μή, in Matt. *Did.* Barn. οὐ (so O.T.). Probably Jews and Christians alike used the Decalogue in forms which

shalt not forswear thyself, thou shalt not bear false witness, thou shalt not slander, thou shalt not bear malice. 4. Thou shalt not be double-minded nor double-tongued : for a double tongue is a deadly snare. 5. Thy word shall not be false, nor empty, but fulfilled in deed. 6. Thou shalt not be covetous, nor extortionate, nor a hypocrite, nor spiteful, nor arrogant. Thou shalt not take evil counsel against thy neighbour. 7.

varied much in wording from one another, and we cannot say with confidence that any particular addition was original in the writer where we find it.—" Thou shalt not forswear thyself " (οὐκ ἐπιορκήσεις) is in *Ap. Ch. Ord.* and Matt. v. 33, not in Barn. It is a paraphrase of Lev. xix. 12 LXX, etc.—To " bear malice " (μνησικακήσεις) Barn. adds "against thy brother," a reminiscence of Zech. vii. 10 (see Introd., § 2). This may be original.

4. *double-minded* (διγνώμων). Cf. Jas. i. 8, iv. 8 (δίψυχος), and below iv. 4 (διψυχήσεις, a late word). The whole section is in *Ap. Ch. Ord.*, Barn., but the latter separates the two halves, and for " a double tongue " reads " the mouth."

5. *fulfilled in deed* (μεμεστωμένος πράξει), a very singular phrase which is not good Greek; omitted in *Ap. Ch. Ord.* Barnabas has : " The word of God shall not come forth from thee in the uncleanness of some."

6. *arrogant*. The parallel *Ap. Const.* vii. 5, adds a quotation from Prov. iii. 34 LXX (= Jas. iv. 6b, 1 Pet. v. 5b.); so Pseudo-Ignatius, *Hero* 5.

7. This is based on Lev. xix. 17 f. LXX, which has " thou shalt not hate " and " reprove " (ἐλέγξεις), and " thou shalt love thy neighbour as thyself." Lightfoot refers also to Jude 22, but this is too far away, though two uncials there have ἐλέγχετε (Westcott-Hort, *Notes on Select Readings*, p. 107). The *Ap. Ch. Ord.* adds " on some thou shalt have mercy " from Jude (Hilgenfeld inserts it here). Probably the original *Two Ways*, even if a Christian document, had no reference to Jude.—For " some thou shalt love " Barn. 19 has : " thou shalt love thy neighbour." See also Introd., § 2.

III] THE DIDACHE 7

Thou shalt hate no man, but some thou shalt reprove, and for some thou shalt pray, and some thou shalt love more than thy soul.

CHAPTER III

1. My child, flee from all evil and from all that is like it. 2. Be not wrathful: for wrath guideth to murder: nor a zealot, nor contentious, nor quick to anger: for from all these things murders are begotten. 3. My child, be not lustful, for lust guideth to fornication: nor a filthy talker, nor one of high looks: for from all these things adulteries are begotten. 4. My child, be

III. 1. So *Ap. Ch. Ord.* (Syr.) 7, but the Sahidic has "and hate all evil" for "and . . . like it." Cf. 1 Thess. v. 22, where see G. Milligan's note and R.V. If the *Didache* writer is quoting this verse, he takes εἶδος as "appearance" (so A.V.); but in that case it is not "semblance" as opposed to "reality," but "visible form."—Barnabas has nothing of our §§ 1-6, and Dr Robinson (*Donn. Lect.*, p. 62) suggests that *Did.* is quoting a Jewish or Early Christian apocryphon. But why not a version of the *Two Ways*?

2, 3. After "murder" *Ap. Ch. Ord.* adds "for wrath is a male demon," and after "fornication" adds "for lust is a female demon," and inserts several sentences. The "zealot" is a fanatic.

3. *of high looks* (ὑψηλόφθαλμος), not found before *Did.*; in classical Gk. ὑψηλόφρων. *Ap. Const.* vii. 6 has ῥιψόφθαλμος "casting lewd glances," and also ὑψηλόφρων.

4. *augur* (οἰωνοσκόπος), lit. "bird-watcher." Cf. Lev. xix. 26 LXX. The augur divined by the flight of birds, the enchanter used magical words and amulets. See also v. 1.

not an augur : for it guideth to idolatry : nor an enchanter, nor an astrologer, nor a purifier, nor do thou consent to look on these things : for

astrologer, lit. "mathematician"; *Ap. Ch. Ord.* "teacher of strange and pagan teachings." "Mathematicus" is so used in Juvenal (vi. 561, xiv. 248), Tacitus (*Hist.* i. 22), and Tertullian (*Apol.* 43); Aulus Gellius (I ix. 6) says it was a vulgar use of the word. The Greek word retained the sense of "astronomer" (Philo, *de Mut. Nom.* i. 589 [§ 10]; Plutarch, *de Facie in orbe lunae* ix. *de Is. et Os.* xli.; Porphyry, *Vita Plotini* 15); perhaps this is the first instance of the use of the *Greek* word as "astrologer." The Church was always on its guard against magic, no doubt with good reason. The Emperor Hadrian in his probably genuine *Epistle to Servianus* (Lightfoot, *Ignat. and Polyc.* i. 480, ed. 2) says: "Nemo Christianorum presbyter non mathematicus, non haruspex, non aliptes." This need not be taken too seriously, but it shows how great was the danger.

purifier. This word refers to heathen lustrations. They were much practised in the nursery; Augustine (*Conf.* i. 7), speaking of the faults of childhood, says: "Mothers and nurses say that they make atonement [for these faults] by what remedies I know not."—The derived *Ap. Const.* vii. 6, has "purifier of thy son." The word may refer to purifying by fire as in Lev. xviii. 21, Deut. xviii. 10.

With this section compare the lists of occupations forbidden to candidates for baptism in the Church Orders from the time of Hippolytus onwards. Thus in the "*So-called Egyptian Church Order*," which has with good reason been assigned to that father (early third century) the list (Connolly, p. 182) includes "a stargazer, and a diviner by the sun, or soothsayer, or interpreter of dreams, or seducer of the people . . . or a maker of potions" (the Latin is here wanting). The *Testament of our Lord* (ii. 2; *c.* A.D. 350) has "diviner, magician, necromancer . . . charmer, astrologer, interpreter of dreams, sorcerer, gatherer of the people, stargazer, diviner by idols." The lists in the *Canons of Hippolytus* (can. xv, ed. Achelis § 76; fourth century?) and *Ap. Const.* viii. 32 are similar.

THE DIDACHE

from all these things idolatry is begotten. 5. My child, be not a liar : for the lie guideth to theft : nor a lover of money, nor vainglorious : for from all these things thefts are begotten. 6. My child, be not a murmurer : for it guideth to blasphemy : nor self-willed; nor evil-minded; for from all these things blasphemies are begotten. 7. But be meek, for the meek shall inherit the earth. 8. Be longsuffering, and merciful, and

5. *My child . . . theft*, so *Ap. Ch. Ord.* 11 (but the Sahidic and Bohairic have " blasphemy " for " theft "). Clement of Alexandria (*Strom.* i. 20) quotes this saying prefaced by : " It is such an one that is by Scripture called a thief; it is therefore said." He seems to quote it as Scripture. See Introd., § 5. Dr. Robinson (*Donn. Lect.*, p. 62) suggests some last apocryphal work as the common source of Clement and the *Didache*.

nor a lover of money, omitted by *Ap. Ch. Ord.*

6. *blasphemies*. So *Ap. Ch. Ord.* (Syr.), but Sah. "quarrels."

self-willed. In *Ap. Ch. Ord.* " proud and lifted up."

7. From Matt. v. 5, and so *Ap. Ch. Ord.* 11 (Sah.), but Syr. " inherit the kingdom of heaven." Barnabas omits the quotation from Matt., and has at an earlier stage, but just before the reference to Isaiah (below, § 8) : " Thou shalt be meek, thou shall be quiet." Thus some current forms of the *Two Ways* cannot have had the quotation from Matt. After " be meek " the parallel *Ap. Const.* vii. 7 adds " as Moses and David " (cf. Pseudo-Ignatius, *Eph.* 10). The *Test. of our Lord* (ii. 1) requires candidates for baptism to be "not contentious, quiet, meek, not speaking vain things, or despisers, or foul speakers, or leaders astray, or ridicule mongers."

8. *longsuffering*. *Ap. Const.* vii. 8 quotes Prov. xiv. 29. cited also in Pseudo-Ignatius, *Hero* 5.

quiet, trembling at the words, from Isa. lxvi. 2 LXX, nearly, So Barnabas and *Ap. Ch. Ord.*, agreeing with the *Didache* as against Isaiah.

harmless, and quiet, and good, and trembling always at the words that thou didst hear. 9. Thou shalt not exalt thyself, nor give boldness to thy soul. Thy soul shall not cleave to the lofty, but with the just and lowly shalt thou walk. 10. The providences that befall thee thou shalt welcome as good, knowing that without God nothing cometh to pass.

9. *nor give boldness to thy soul.* So Barn. 19, which, however, adds three clauses between this one and "thou shalt not exalt thyself." The following part of this section comes in Barnabas a good deal later. *Ap. Ch. Ord.* 11, agrees with *Did.* in combining the whole section, but apparently its author did not understand "give boldness to thy soul," and it has this conflation : " Thou shalt not exalt thyself, neither shalt thou give thy soul with the haughty, but with the just and lowly shalt thou walk," and goes on to our § 10. Thus the *Ap. Ch. Ord.* cannot be derived from Barnabas.

10. So Barn. 19 verbatim, but with ἄνευ for *Did.* ἄτερ; so also *Ap. Ch. Ord.* 11; for the idea cf. Ecclus. ii. 4. The " providences " (ἐνεργήματα) are the "dispensations" or (Lightfoot) "accidents "; the operations of God's providence. This saying is quoted by Origen (*de Princ.* III ii. 7) : " Holy Scripture teaches us to receive all that happens as sent by God, knowing that without him no event occurs." As Origen had just quoted Barnabas by name in § 4, this also is probably from him rather than from the *Didache*.

CHAPTER IV

1. My child, night and day shalt thou remember him that speaketh to thee the word of

IV. 1. *night and day*. So Barn. 19, *Ap. Ch. Ord.* 12; *Ap. Const.* vii. 9 has "day and night." The former refers to the Eastern custom of beginning the new day at sunset, the latter to the Roman custom of beginning it at midnight. The usage in the New Testament and in early Christian writers varies, the same writer being often inconsistent (Wordsworth, *Min. of Grace* vi., p. 305; Cooper-Maclean, *Test. of our Lord*, p. 159).

speaketh . . . God, so *Ap. Ch. Ord.* 12, from Heb. xiii. 7 (see Intr., § 2); so also Barn. 19, but with "Lord" (anarthrous) for "God." The *Ap. Ch. Ord.* adds: "and is to thee the cause of life and giveth thee the seal [baptism] in Christ, him shalt thou love as the apple of thine eye; remember him night and day and honour him as God, for where the Lordship is spoken of, there is the Lord. Thou shalt seek his face daily and the rest of the saints, that thou mayest find rest in their words . . . for if the Lord has vouchsafed to give thee spiritual food and [spiritual, Sah.] drink and life eternal [see below on x. 3] at his hands, much more art thou bound to present to him perishable and temporal food," etc. [quoting 1 Cor. ix. 9, 7]. These remarks about the support of the ministry are not in *Did.* or Barn., but the latter, unlike *Did.*, has: "Thou shalt love as the apple of thine eye [cf. *Ap. Ch. Ord.*] every one that speaketh unto thee the word of the Lord. Thou shalt remember the *day of judgment* night and day, and thou shalt seek out day by day (καθ' ἑκάστην ἡμέραν, = *Did.* καθ' ἡ.) the faces of the saints," and then goes on differently, making the "saints" the Christians to whom the hearer is exhorted to minister. It is hardly conceivable that this text was that of the original *Two Ways*, or that *Ap. Ch. Ord.* or *Did.* are here deriving from Barnabas. It is much more probable that the

12   THE DIDACHE   [IV

God, and thou shalt honour him as the Lord, for in him by whom the Lordship is spoken of is the Lord. 2. And daily shalt thou seek out the faces of the saints, that thou mayest rest on their words. 3. Thou shalt not desire division, but shalt set at peace them that strive : thou shalt judge justly; thou shalt not regard persons, when thou rebukest for transgressions. 4. Thou shalt not be double-minded, whether it shall be or not. 5. Be not one that holdeth out his hands

remembering of the preacher by night as well as by day struck Barnabas as an exaggeration, and that he therefore changed it to a remembering of the day of judgment.

the Lordship . . . the Lord. So *Ap. Ch. Ord.* 12, the Syriac preserving the paronomasia; Barn. omits. " The Lordship" apparently means "the nature and work of the Lord." *Ap. Const.* vii. 9 has "for where the teaching of God is, there God is present," the writer probably finding " Lordship "difficult to understand.

3. *desire* (ποθήσεις). Hilgenfeld conjectures "make" (ποιήσεις), as Barn. and *Ap. Ch. Ord.* (Barn. separates the clauses of the section). The verb εἰρηνεύω may be transitive " to set at peace " as here (cf. 1 Macc. vi. 60, " to make peace "), or intransitive " to be at peace " as in the N.T. In Barn. 19 we have εἰρηνεύσεις δὲ μαχομένους συναγωγών, which may mean " set at peace them that strive, bringing [them] together," or (as Robinson) " be at peace, bringing together them that strive." But the last is a somewhat forced translation.

4. *be double-minded* (διψυχήσεις), *i. e.* doubt, hesitate (so Barn.); *Ap. Const.* vii. 11 interprets by inserting " in thy prayer." So *Ap. Ch. Ord.* 13 : " In thy prayer [or prayers] thou shalt not hesitate which shall be, Yea or Nay," or (Sah.) "thinking whether what thou askest will be or not." This seems to be the meaning in *Did.* See on ii. 4.

5. Paraphrased from Ecclus. iv. 31. For " shutteth " (συσπῶν, so Barn., *Ap. Ch. Ord.*), *Ap. Const.* vii. 12 has συστέλλων " restraining," and so Ecclus. συνεσταλμένη.

IV] THE DIDACHE 13

to receive and shutteth them for giving. 6. If
thou have aught in thy hands, thou shalt give a
ransom for thy sins. 7. Thou shalt not doubt
to give, nor shalt thou murmur when thou givest :
for thou shalt know who is the good requiter of
the reward. 8. Thou shalt not turn away from
him that hath need, but shalt share all things
with thy brother, and shalt not say that aught
is thine own: for, if ye are partners in the
eternal, how much more are ye partners in the

6. *in* (διά) *thy hands*. Or (Lightfoot) "passing through
thy hands"; or we might join on to what follows : "by
thy hands thou shalt give," etc. Barnabas adds to the
clauses about remembering the day of judgment (above,
§ 1) "thou shalt work with thy hands for a ransom for thy
sins." This, again, must be secondary. The reference is
to Dan. iv. 27.

7. *Murmur* (γογγύσεις), so Barn., *Ap. Ch. Ord.*; in iii. 6
we have "a murmurer" (γόγγυσος), both being late words.
Cf. 1 Pet. iv. 9 (in connection with hospitality).

8. *turn away*, cf. Matt. v. 42; "thine own" comes from
Acts iv. 32 (so Barn. 19, *Ap. Ch. Ord.* 13). See Introd., § 2.

eternal. Rather "imperishable" (or "immortal"), to
correspond with "perishable" (τῷ ἀθανάτῳ—τοῖς θνητοῖς);
Barnabas has ἀφθάρτῳ—φθαρτοῖς. For the idea cf. Rom. xv.
27; *Ap. Const.* vii. 12 omits this parallel and gives other words.

At the end of this section the *Ap. Ch. Ord.* breaks off, and
omits the rest of this chapter and the Way of Death. The
remainder of that work is quite independent of the *Didache*.
The writer had before him probably a mutilated copy of an
independent version of the *Two Ways*, which did not contain
the Sermon on the Mount section. The *Didache* form of
the tract seems to be more original than that of *Ap. Ch.
Ord.*, which appears to have added phrases to its source.
This is much more probable than that the *Didache* omitted
them. The method of addition in *Ap. Ch. Ord.* is exactly
parallel to the way in which *Ap. Const.* (vii. 1-32) treated
the *Didache*.

14   THE DIDACHE   [IV

perishable? 9. Thou shalt not remove thy hand from thy son, or from thy daughter, but from youth up shalt teach them the fear of God. 10. Thou shalt not command thy servant or thy handmaiden, who hope on the same God, in thy bitterness, lest they fear not the God who is over both : for he cometh not to call according to respect of persons, but on those whom the Spirit prepared. 11. And ye, servants, shall be subject to your masters, as to a type of God, in modesty and fear. 12. Thou shalt hate all hypocrisy, and all that is not pleasing to the Lord. 13. Thou shalt not forsake the commandments of the Lord, but shalt keep what thou didst receive, neither adding thereto nor

9–14. These sections are mostly found in Barnabas, though the order is different; § 9 f. are almost verbatim as Barn., though there separated by a considerable interval; § 11 is nearly as Barn., where it precedes our § 10; § 12 is almost as Barn., where it comes much earlier, but there the two parts of it are inverted; so is § 13, but in Barn. the first clause is very widely separated from the last two; § 14 is the end of the " Way of Light " (*i. e.* of Life) in Barn. also. The fact that some of these clauses come early in Barn., and yet do not occur in *Ap. Ch. Ord.*, is another argument against the latter being derived from the former.

10. *on those*. Either " to call on those whom," or " he cometh to those," etc.

11. *as to a type of God*, so Barn. 19. Cf. Ignatius, *Magn.* 6 (the bishop a type of God, the presbyters a type of the apostolic college), *Trall.* 3. The MS has " our masters " by error; see on x. 2, xiv. 1.

13. *neither adding . . . away*, a paraphrase of Deut. iv. 2, the same verbs being used; cf. also Deut. xii. 32, Rev. xxii. 18 f.

v] THE DIDACHE 15

taking aught away. 14. Thou shalt confess thy transgressions in church, and shalt not come to thy prayer in an evil conscience. This is the Way of Life.

CHAPTER V

1. But the Way of Death is this: first of all it is wicked and full of curse : murders, adulteries,

14. *in church* (ἐν ἐκκλησίᾳ), omitted in Barn. and *Ap. Const.* vii. 14. The meaning is "the Christian assembly." Cf. Clement of Alexandria, *Strom.* v. 29: "By church I do not mean just now the place, but the assembly of the elect;" also 1 Cor. xi. 18, where again the article is omitted as the phrase is a familiar one (cf. Acts xvi. 13, and W. M. Ramsay, *St Paul the Traveller*, ed. 6, p. 213). For public confession in the Early Church see G. Mead, art. "Exomologesis" in *Dict. Chr. Ant.* i. 644, and F. E. Brightman in Swete's *Essays*, pp. 353-380; cf. Tertullian, *de Poen.* 9 ff.

The Way of Death.—V. 1. Here *Did.*, Barn., and *Ap. Const.* vii. 18 are very close together, the last having very few additions. But in Barn. 20 it is called "the Way of the Black One" (Satan); see note on *Did.* xvi. 2. In Barn. 18 it is "the Way of Darkness."

wicked. In Barn. 20 "crooked." For "full of a curse," *Ap. Const.* has, "In it is ignorance of God and the introduction of many gods" (var. lect., "many evils and disorders [? θολῶν] and disturbances"). Barn. adds: "for it is a way of eternal death with punishment, wherein are the things that destroy their souls."—The list of sins in Barn. differs a good deal in order, and omits some of those in *Did*. At the end comes "absence of the fear of God" (ἀφοβία θεοῦ); so the Latin *Two Ways:* Deum non timentes. But in *Ap. Const.* ἀφοβία (without θεοῦ) also ends the list, which otherwise very closely follows *Did.* Hence we may conjecture

lusts, fornications, thefts, idolatries, witchcrafts, sorceries, ravenings, false witnessings, hypocrisies, a double heart, guile, arrogance, malice, self-will, covetousness, filthy talking, jealousy, boldness, pride, boasting. 2. Persecutors of good men, haters of truth, loving a lie, not knowing the recompense of righteousness, not cleaving to good, nor to just judgment, watching not for that which is good, but for that which is evil : from whom meekness is far off and patience, loving vanity, hunting after reward, not pitying the poor man, not sorrowing over him that is weighed down by sorrow, knowing not him that made them, murderers of children, destroyers of God's handiwork, turning aside from him that

---

that " absence of fear " has dropped out of the latter, perhaps by a clerical error, and that the original *Two Ways* had it. In *Clem. Hom.* i. 18 ἀφοβία is included in the list of sins.

2. The change from the abstract sins to the concrete sinners is the same in Barn. 20; but *Ap. Const.* continues the abstract till he is obliged to make the change by the quotation from Rom. xii. 9 "cleaving to good" (see Introd., § 2).

judgment. Barn. adds " paying no heed to the widow and the orphan."

watching . . . good. Barn. has " watching not for the fear of God "; this must be secondary.

sorrowing . . . sorrow. Or " toiling for him that is oppressed with toil " (Lightfoot). Barn. inserts " ready in slander."

The last clause of this section is not in Barn., and was probably the composition of our author; but he has suddenly diverged into the plural " my children." This shows that he is making use of an older document which used the singular. See on vii 1.

THE DIDACHE

hath need, grinding down the afflicted, advocates of the rich, unjust judges of the poor, steeped in sin. May ye be delivered, my children, from all these.

CHAPTER VI

1. See that no man lead thee astray from this Way of the doctrine, for he teacheth thee with-

VI. This is a sort of epilogue to the *Two Ways*, still addressed to the single disciple, and leading on to the chapters which follow. This method of making a connecting-link is found elsewhere. In the *Eg. Ch. Ord.* (Connolly, p. 175) there is a preface joining the (Hippolytean?) treatise " Of gifts " to the canons which follow, though that treatise is not now attached to them. The *Ap. Const.* has a similar connecting-link in viii. 3, joining ch. 1, 2 ("On Gifts") to ch. 4, the beginning of the ecclesiastical regulations. Similarly the *Test. of our Lord* has chapters (i. 14b-18) which connect the apocalyptic prelude with the main part of the book; in these chapters there is a reflection of the preface in *Eg. Ch. Ord.*—Of this chapter of *Did.* the *Ap. Const.* has preserved only the injunction to abstain from things offered to idols. The *Didache* advises, but does not command, asceticism; the writer of *Ap. Const.* is always afraid of the over-asceticism of his own day.—The first section of this chapter seems to belong to the *Two Ways;* the Latin version of the latter has it, and adds a few more sentences (*Journ. of Theol. Stud.* xiii. 342). This Latin version, published by Schlecht (see Intr., § 10), proves the independence of the *Two Ways*. It has not got our i. 3-6, adds " light and darkness " to our " life and death," has the reference to the angels, and concludes with a Christian doxology; but " is, in fact, very little removed from its Jewish original " (Wordsworth, *Min. of Grace*, p. 441). See Intr., § 2.

out God. 2. For, if thou canst bear the whole yoke of the Lord, thou shalt be perfect; but, if thou canst not, do what thou canst. 3. And as regards eating, bear what thou canst, but of meat offered to idols beware thou diligently: for it is a worship of dead gods.

CHAPTER VII

1. And concerning baptism, baptize ye thus. Having first declared all these things, baptize into

2. *the whole yoke of the Lord.* Cf. Acts xv. 10, and possibly Matt. xi. 29 ("my yoke"). But in Acts the distinction is between Jewish and Gentile converts rather than, as here, between a higher and lower following of an ideal.

3. *And as regards eating* (περὶ δὲ τῆς βρώσεως). So 1 Cor. viii. 4 (περὶ τ.β.). Our author is fond of beginning sections with περὶ δέ (cf. vii. 1, ix. 1-3, xi. 2), as also we find in 1 Cor. vii. 1, 25, viii. 1 [4], xii. 1, xvi. 1, 12 (J. A. Robinson in *Journ. of Theol. Stud.* xiii. 344).—The distinction of clean and unclean meats is not here in question. What the author means is that it is better to eat no meat at all, but that in any case the Christian is bound by the decrees of Acts xv. 20.

dead gods (θεῶν νεκρῶν). So the *Ancient Homily* (Pseudo-Clem. Rom., 2 *Cor.* ii. 3): "We do not sacrifice to the dead gods" (τοῖς νεκροῖς θεοῖς); and Melito, *Discourse to Antoninus* (ed. Otto, *Corp. Apol. Chr.* ix. 425): "They adore the images of dead kings." The tomb of Zeus was said to be shown in Crete (Athenagoras, *Embassy* 30, ed. Otto vii. 158). Cf. also *Ep. to Diognetus* 2.

Baptism.—VII. 1. Hitherto our author has used the singular, addressing a single disciple (but see on v. 2); after this he addresses the whole community in the plural. This is one of many indications that he incorporated a previously

VII] THE DIDACHE 19

the name of the Father, and of the Son, and of
the Holy Ghost in living water. 2. But if thou

composed tract, that on the *Two Ways*, into his work.
Although the whole community is now addressed, the
meaning cannot be, here and elsewhere, that the whole
body baptizes, ordains, etc. Officials are specially mentioned
(*e. g.* x. 7, xi, xv).

baptize in the name. Rather "into (εἰs) the name," from
Matt. xx. 19; so in § 3 the meaning is "pour water thrice
. . . [baptizing] into the name," etc. (cf. ix. 5). See the discussion between Dr F. H. Chase and Dr J. A. Robinson on the
meaning of the baptismal command, in *Journ. of Theol. Stud.*
vi. 500 ff., vii. 186 ff., viii. 161 ff.—It is going too far to
suggest that the *only* preparatory teaching for baptism was
that given in ch. i-vi; wherever the Three Names were used
there must have been some definite instruction as to their
meaning.

in living water (ἐν ὕδατι ζῶντι), *i. e.*, probably, running water,
as Gen. xxvi. 19, Lev. xiv. 5, 50 LXX. So *Eg. Ch. Ord.*:
"It shall be either such as flows into the tank of baptism,
or is caused to flow down upon it" (Connolly, p. 183); but
this is relaxed if there is a scarcity of water. So also *Test.
of our Lord* (ii. 8): "let the water be pure and flowing;"
and the *Canons of Hippolytus* (can. xix, ed. Achelis § 112),
where Dr Burkitt has shown that it is not sea water, but a
flowing stream, that is meant (*Journ. of Theol. Stud.* i. 279).
The rule in these Church Orders seems to be that the water
is to flow into and out of the font. So also the *Clementine
Recognitions* iii. 67, vi. 15 "ever flowing waters," and *Clem.
Homilies* xi. 26 "living water," xi. 35 "ever flowing"
(ἀέναον). Yet in the *Ap. Const.* vii. 22, derived from this
passage of the *Didache*, the "living water" is omitted.
Baptism in the sea would satisfy the requirements (cf. *Clem.
Recog.* iv. 32, "water of the fountain or river or even sea"),
but it is unlikely that the phrase "living water" has any
reference to fresh, as opposed to salt, water; as a matter of
fact we read of baptism in the sea in the *Clem. Homilies*
(xiv. 1), and Tertullian says that "it makes no difference
whether a man be washed [baptized] in a sea, or a pool,
or a stream, or a fount, a lake, or a trough (*de Bapt.* 4);

have not living water, baptize into other water; and, if thou canst not in cold, in warm. 3. But if thou have neither, pour water thrice upon

cf. the suggestion by some that the apostles were baptized in the sea (*Ibid.* 12).—It is very unlikely that the *Didache* derives its "living water" from John iv. 10 f., vii. 38.

if . . . cold, no doubt in case of sickness.

3. *But if . . . pour water, i. e.* if there is not a sufficient quantity. Elsewhere we read of baptism by affusion only in cases of the sick, that is, in "clinical" baptisms, though a common method of baptizing was for the candidate to stand with his feet in the water while the minister poured water on his head; see the illustration from the catacombs in W. B. Marriott's article "Baptism" in *Dict. Chr. Ant.* i. 168*b*. Clinical baptism is not in view in *Did.*; it was discouraged in the Early Church as showing that it was received only through fear of death; one so baptized could not, in some places, be ordained priest, or to any clerical office (Cornelius, A.D. 251 or 252, in Eusebius, *H.E.* vi. 43, Council of Neocæsarea in Cappadocia, between A.D. 314 and 325, can. 12); though the council of Laodicea in Phrygia attaches no stigma to those thus baptized (can. 47, *c.* A.D. 380), and that of Neocæsarea makes an exception if they are zealous and faithful, or if there is a scarcity of men (for the office). Cyprian says (*Ep.* lxix. [lxxv.] 13) that clinical baptism is valid, but that if the baptized recover they should be "baptized" (*i. e.* confirmed?). We cannot infer from this that the *Didache*, which shows no doubt about the matter, is later than Cyprian. The cases are not parallel. Here we have, not persons who endeavour to avoid Church discipline or seek baptism unworthily, but the geographical difficulty of a scarcity of water. *Ap. Const.* vii. 22 omits these provisions and exceptions, but, in inserting unctions into the baptismal rite (which, rather strangely, are entirely absent in *Did.*), transposes the exception to the anointing: "If (thou have) neither oil nor unguent (μύρον), the water suffices both for the anointing, and the seal, and the confession." —Irenæus (*Haer.* I xxi. 4) says that some Gnostics baptized by affusion.—The word "thrice" in *Did.* shows that trine *immersion* was the normal custom,

VII] THE DIDACHE 21

the head into the name of Father, Son, and Holy Ghost. 4. And before the baptism let the baptizer and him that is baptized fast, and such others as can : and thou shalt enjoin the baptized to fast for one or two days before.

4. The pre-baptismal fast of the candidates seems to have been universal in the Early Church; but the fast by the baptizer and others, as here, is not quite so common. For the fast by the candidates, see Justin Martyr, *Apol.* i. 61 (all the community fast also); Tertullian, *de Bapt.* 20; *Clem. Hom.* iii. 73, xi. 35, xiii. 11 (in § 12 Peter also fasts with Mattidia and her sons); *Clem. Recog.* iii. 67, vi. 15, vii. 34, 37 (at least one day : Peter and the sons fast also); and most of the Church Orders—the *Eg. Ch. Ord.*, on the Friday before Easter, Easter Day being the normal day for baptism (Connolly, p. 183; the Latin is wanting); the *Test. of our Lord* (ii. 6), on the Friday and the Saturday; the *Canons of Hippolytus* (can. xix, ed. Achelis § 106) on the Friday; this last work speaks (can. xix, § 150) of others fasting with the neophytes until they make their communion. In *Ap. Const.* vii. 22 the fast of the candidates is retained, though its duration is not mentioned, but that of the baptizer and others is dropped; the writer gives reasons why our Lord fasted after baptism rather than before it. The *Didache* writer mentions no fixed season or day for baptism; he does not use the words "catechize" or "catechumen," nor does he refer to infant baptism, as the Church Orders do.—For "thou shalt enjoin" the MS has "thou enjoinest" (κελεύεις for κελεύσεις).—For possible reasons for the omission of any mention of confirmation, see F. E. Brightman in Swete's *Essays*, p. 378 *n*. (above, Introd., § 10).

THE DIDACHE [VIII

CHAPTER VIII

1. And let not your fasts be with the hypocrites : for they fast on the second and fifth days

Fasting and Prayer.—VIII. 1. *the hypocrites*. From Matt. vi. 16, but here it means all Jews. For the Jewish fasts on Monday and Thursday see Epiphanius, *Haer*. xvi. They were due to the belief that Moses went up to and came down from Mount Sinai on those days ; cf. Luke xviii. 12 " twice in the week." Hermas (*Sim*. v. 1) speaks of keeping a fast which he calls a " station," but does not say on which day of the week it was. The mention of Wednesday and Friday (lit. " the Preparation," παρασκευή) in *Did*. perhaps shows that the author knew of the historical events of the Passion. These two fast days are mentioned by Tertullian—he calls them " station days," by a military metaphor meaning that the Church is on guard, and " half-fasts " (*de Orat*. 19, *de Jejun*. 2, 13 f.)—Clement of Alexandria (*Strom*. vii. 12), the *Older Didascalia* (v. 14, Funk, i. 276), Peter of Alexandria (*Ep. canon*. 15, early fourth century), the *Canons of Hippolytus* can. xx, ed. Achelis § 154), Epiphanius (*Haer*. lxv. 6, *Exp. Fid*. 21), Rufinus' translation of Origen *in Lev*. Hom. x. (we can only take this as fourth century evidence, the original Greek being lost), *Ap. Const*. v. 15, 20, vii. 23 (the latter gives as an alternative " or the five days," *i. e*. Monday to Thursday inclusive), *Apost. Canons* 69 [68], *Arabic Didascalia* 38 (derived from the *Test. of our Lord*, which, however, does not mention these days), and Pseudo-Ignatius (*Philipp*. 13; *c*. A.D. 400). In the *Edessene Canons* (*c*. A.D. 350) these are days for public prayer, but the fast is not mentioned. For the reasons given for these fasts, and for further information, see *Prayer Book Dictionary* (London, 1912), p. 820a, and J. Wordsworth, *Ministry of Grace*, p. 327.—Nothing is here said of Easter, or of the fast of at least two days which was customarily observed before it (a pregnant woman was allowed to fast on the Saturday only, *e. g*. in *Eg. Ch. Ord*., Connolly, p. 190, *Test. of our Lord* ii. 20).—The construction in the Greek is curious. After the first " fast " the dative

VIII] THE DIDACHE 23

of the week: but do ye fast on the fourth and on Friday. 2. Neither pray ye as do the hypocrites, but as the Lord commanded in his gospel, so pray ye: Our Father which art in heaven, hallowed be thy name, thy kingdom come, thy

is used, but after the second the accusative—νηστεύσατε τετράδα καὶ παρασκευήν; cf. perhaps the *Oxyrhynchus Logia* ii. νηστεύσητε τὸν κόσμον . . . σαββατίσητε τὸ σάββατον (" fast from the world . . . keep the sabbath ").

2. *his gospel.* So xi. 3, xv. 3 f. "the gospel." The use of the word is an intermediate one, between the written record and the thing preached. The same thing is found in Ignatius (see Lightfoot's note on Ignat., *Phil.* 5, 8; ii. pp. 261, 271).—For the connection of fasting and prayer cf. Acts xiii. 3, Matt. vi. 5-18.—The text of the Lord's Prayer is almost exactly derived from Matt., and does not depend on Luke xi. 2-4; but it has ἐν τῷ οὐρανῷ for ἐν τοῖς οὐρανοῖς, ἐλθέτω for ἐλθάτω, τὴν ὀφειλήν for τὰ ὀφειλήματα, and ἀφίεμεν for ἀφήκαμεν. The doxology here is a liturgical addition to the prayer, and is not in the true text of the gospels; it and the other doxologies in *Did.* are less developed than those in *Eg. Ch. Ord.* and the other Church Orders derived from it, which have such as the following : " Jesus Christ, through whom be to thee glory and power and honour, to the Father and the Son with the Holy Ghost, now and for ever, Amen." Here "the kingdom" is omitted, as it is by Gregory of Nyssa (F. H. Chase, *The Lord's Prayer in the Early Church*, Cambridge, 1891, p. 174) and one or two other authorities, but it is inserted in *Ap. Const.* vii. 24. The Curetonian Syriac at Matt. vi. 13 has: "for thine is the kingdom and the glory for ever and ever, Amen "; the Sinaitic Syriac is here wanting. In *Did.* the doxology does not belong exclusively to the Lord's Prayer: see x. 5, and cf. ix. 2, 3, 4, x. 2, 4. For the history of the doxology see Westcott-Hort, *Notes on Select Readings*, p. 8 (*New Test. in Greek*, vol. ii.).

from evil. This is perhaps the interpretation of *Did.*, rather than " from the Evil One "; cf. x. 5, " deliver her from all evil " (ἀπὸ παντὸς πονηροῦ).

will be done on earth, as it is in heaven. Give us this day our daily bread, and forgive us our debt, as we also forgive our debtors, and lead us not into temptation, but deliver us from evil. For thine is the power and the glory for ever. 3. Thrice in the day pray ye thus.

CHAPTER IX

1. And as regards the eucharist, give thanks

3. *Thrice in the day;* so *Ap. Const.* vii. 24. The reference is probably to the three hours of prayer (Dan. vi. 10, Ps. lv. 17, Acts ii. 15, x. 3, 16). The number increased greatly as time went on. Tertullian (*de Orat.* 25, *de Jejun.* 10) and Clement of Alexandria (*Strom.* vii. 7 [40]) mention three, the third, sixth, and ninth hours. But Cyprian has six (*de Orat. Dom.*, 34 ff.), and the Church Orders six, seven, or eight (see the present editor's *Ancient Church Orders*, p. 60 f.). This is a sign of early date in the *Didache*.

Eucharist (Agape?).—IX. 1. It has been disputed whether this chapter refers to the eucharist proper, or to the agape. We notice (1) that the cup comes before the bread; (2) that there is no reference to the Last Supper, or to the death of our Lord, or to the remission of sins, or to the resurrection; (3) that this chapter refers to a meal in which the partakers are " filled " (x. 1, see note), and which is given them " to enjoy " (x. 3); (4) that after the thanksgiving which follows the meal there is a " fencing of the tables " (x. 6); (5) and that this is followed by an extemporaneous " giving of thanks " by the " prophets " (x. 7). In favour of the reference being to the eucharist proper we have the name itself in ix. 1, περὶ δὲ τῆς εὐχαριστίας, and the absence otherwise of any description of the eucharist save the references, above mentioned, in x. 6, 7, and those in xiv. 1–3. In favour of the reference in ix. 1–x. 5 being to the agape we have the fact

THE DIDACHE

in this manner. 2. *First for the cup.* We thank thee, our Father, for the holy vine of David, thy

that the agape would otherwise not be described at all, though the writer clearly recognized that institution (xi. 9), and, even if he depended only on the New Testament, he would learn of its existence from that source; also the facts that the words "after ye are filled" can be naturally interpreted only of a regular meal, and that the "fencing of the tables" and the direction to the prophets would otherwise be entirely out of place in the position where they occur; also that the supposed eucharistic prayers of consecration in this chapter would be quite without parallel in Christian antiquity. The balance of probability seems therefore to be with the view that we have here the agape. In that case the writer uses εὐχαριστία as including both the agape and the eucharist proper, just as the most natural interpretation of Ignatius' "agape" in *Smyrn.* 8 is that it includes both rites. It is unlikely that εὐχαριστία in *Did.* is untechnical, and merely means "thanksgiving." See for divergent views article "Agape" in Hastings' *Encycl. of Religion and Ethics*, i. 168 f. These prayers are probably adaptations of Jewish "graces" before meat. If they are not, as is here suggested, agape prayers, but are meant to be used at the eucharist, they are probably to be said by the communicants.

2. *First for the cup.* The cup comes before the bread, and, if the eucharist proper is in question, we may compare 1 Cor. x. 16 ("the cup of blessing") and Luke xxii. 17 ("a cup"; if with some authorities we omit vv. 19c, 20, this is the only cup in that passage). Yet in *Did.* ix. 5, we have the usual order "let none eat nor drink," just as St Paul recurs to it in 1 Cor. xi. 24-28. This, however, is an argument for the agape being referred to, when we compare the *Eg. Ch. Ord.* There we read that at the agape, before they taste and drink anything whatever, it is proper for them to take the cup and give thanks for it, and (then) drink and eat (Connolly, p. 187); the same recurrence to the natural order immediately occurs : " to the catechumens let them give the bread of blessing and the cup."—The derived *Ap. Const.* vii. 25 omits the prayer over the cup altogether.

THE DIDACHE

servant, which thou didst make known to us through Jesus, thy servant. Glory be to thee for ever. 3. And for the broken bread. We

the holy vine of David. The vine is not here, as in John xv. 1, our Lord, but the eucharistic cup. The expression might go some way to show that our author had not read the Fourth Gospel. Clement of Alexandria, however, uses the phrase " vine of David," apparently with some reference to the cup : " It is he that poured wine on our wounded souls, the blood of the vine of David " (*Quis dives* 29); but here, unlike *Did.*, the " vine of David " may equally be our Lord. In any case *Did.* cannot here be borrowing from Clement. Cf. Origen *in Jud.* Hom. vi. § 2 (Lommatsch, xi. 258) : "antequam verae vitis, quae ascendit de radice David, sanguine inebriemur," the idea of which may come from Ps. xxiii. 5 LXX (τὸ ποτήριόν σου μεθύσκον ὡς κράτιστον).

Jesus thy servant (παιδός). This, not " son," must be here the translation of παῖς, as " David thy servant " had just preceded; and so it will be in x. 3. The word comes from Isa. xlii. 1, lii. 13, etc., LXX, and is found in this sense, probably, in Matt. xii. 18 (quoting Isa. xlii. 1, but not from LXX), Acts iii. 13, 26, iv. 27, 30; perhaps in Clem. Rom., *Cor.* 59 (thrice), where τοῦ ἠγαπημένου παιδός seems to refer to Isa. xlii. 1 (cf. Matt. ἀγαπητός); and certainly in Barnabas 6 (quoting Isa. l. 8 f.), 9 (altered from Exod. xv. 26). On the other hand παῖς was taken as "son," apparently in the *Martyrdom of Polycarp* 14 : " Father of thy beloved and blessed Son (παιδός) Jesus Christ," and elsewhere, and certainly in *Ap. Const.* viii. 40 "thy only-begotten Son" (παιδός); see Lightfoot, *Clement* ii. 171. By the phrase παῖς θεοῦ the heathen understood the Christians to mean " Son of God," *e. g.* Libanius (in Socrates, *H.E.* iii. 23) and Celsus (Origen, *c. Cels.* v. 2). It is an archaic phrase, characteristic of ante-Nicene theology, but still found frequently in the liturgy of *Ap. Const.* (viii. 5, 13, 15, 39–41, and so in 48).

3. *broken bread* (κλάσμα), a word not found elsewhere of the eucharistic bread, though the corresponding phrases " breaking of the bread," " to break bread," of the eucharist, are common; see below, xiv. 1, and Acts ii. 42, 46, xx. 7. The action of our Lord at the Last Supper (Matt. xxvi. 26)

THE DIDACHE

thank thee, our Father, for the life and knowledge which thou didst make known to us through Jesus, thy servant. Glory be to thee for ever. 4. As this bread that is broken was

was the same in that respect as the custom at other meals (Luke xxiv. 35, Matt. xiv. 19, xv. 36). All the evangelists use κλάσματα of the broken pieces at the Feedings (*e. g.* Matt. xiv. 20). *Ap. Const.* vii. 25 omits the word; there this prayer is turned (with additions) into a private prayer for a communicant at the eucharist, apparently at the time of receiving (there is a similar prayer to be then said in the *Test. of our Lord* i. 23); but the "fencing of the tables" and Maranatha, and the command to "the presbyter" to celebrate the eucharist (εὐχαριστεῖν) come in very awkwardly in *Ap. Const.*; see above, on ix. 1.

life and knowledge. Cf. Clem. Alex., *Strom.* v. 10 [66]: "for the meat and drink of the divine Word is knowledge of the divine essence," but there is not here an explicit reference to the eucharist; Clement says that "meat is the mystic contemplation." So *Strom.* v. 11 [70]: "our reasonable meat is knowledge," where Clement is quoting Greek philosophy, and does not refer to the eucharist. Cf. John i. 7 "grace and truth"; the knowledge is no mere intellectual acquirement; see also *Did.* x. 2.

made known (ἐγνώρισας), a reference to Acts ii. 28 (from Ps. xvi. 11). This is a more likely source than John xv. 15, xvii. 26.

4. *bread that is broken* (κλάσμα) *was scattered* (διεσκορπισμένον) *upon the mountains.* The participle is found in John xi. 52, of gathering God's scattered children. Sarapion of Thmuis (Introd., § 5) quotes this sentence in his consecration prayer at the eucharist (*Journ. of Theol. Stud.* i. 26): "As this bread (ἄρτος) has been scattered (ἐσκορπισμένος) on (ἐπάνω, so *Did.*) the mountains, and gathered together and became one (εἰς ἕν: *Did.* omits εἰς), so bring together thy holy Church from every nation and every country and every city and village and house, and make one living catholic Church." There can be no doubt that this is a quotation from the *Didache* prayer. The prayer is also quoted in the

E

scattered upon the mountains, and gathered together, and became one, so let thy Church be gathered together from the ends of the earth into thy kingdom : for thine is the glory and the power through Jesus Christ for ever. 5. And

treatise *De Virginitate* (§ 13), the ascription of which to Athanasius has been defended by von der Golz (" T. und Unt." xiv. 2*a*)—he dates it A.D. 320–340. Here it is an ordinary grace before meat, not before the eucharist : " When thou sittest at table and comest to break bread, sign it thrice with the sign of the cross, saying thus, giving thanks, We thank thee, our Father, for thy (*sic*) holy resurrection, for through Jesus thy Son thou hast made it known (ἐγνώρισας) to us, and as this bread on this table was scattered, but brought together and made one thing, so also may thy Church be gathered from the ends of the world into thy kingdom, for thine is the power and the glory for ever and ever, Amen." This prayer substitutes " resurrection " for " life and knowledge " of *Did.*, and " this table " for " the mountains." The parallel *Ap. Const.* vii. 25 omits " on the mountains " altogether. The idea of the one bread of the eucharist collected from many grains is found also in Cyprian, *Ep.* lxiii. [lxii.] 13 (to Cæcilius). Another parallel to this prayer may be seen in the eucharistic invocation in *Eg. Ch. Ord.* (Connolly, p. 176, Hauler, *Verona Fragments*, p. 107, Brightman, *Lit. E. and W.*, p. 190) : " Send thy holy Spirit on the oblation of the holy Church; gathering it together into one (*in unum congregans*) give," etc. [the Verona text, made known in 1900, is here preferable to Ludolf's, used by Brightman in 1896]. For the idea of " one bread " cf. 1 Cor. x. 17.

5. None but the baptized, not even catechumens, were allowed to be present at the agape, nor *a fortiori* at the eucharist proper. In the eucharistic liturgy the catechumens were dismissed after the preparatory part of the service. The prohibition against the presence of the catechumens at the agape is found in the *Eg. Ch. Ord.* (Connolly, p. 187), where the expression " cena dominica " by the context is shown to mean the love-feast ; and so *Test. of our Lord*

THE DIACHE 29

let none eat nor drink of your eucharist, but
they that are baptized into the name of the
Lord; for as touching this the Lord hath said:
Give not that which is holy to the dogs.

CHAPTER X

1. And, after ye are filled, give thanks thus.

ii. 13, *Canons of Hippolytus* can. xxxiii, ed. Achelis § 172
(*agapis κυριακαῖς*).

baptized into the name of the Lord. Thus our author takes
this phrase as equivalent to baptism into the Name of
Father, Son, and Holy Ghost (see vii. 1, 3). The *Ap. Const.*
vii. 5 (which applies this prohibition to the eucharist proper,
see note on ix. 3 above) substitutes "death" for "name,"
baptism into our Lord's death (Rom. vi. 3) being a favourite
theme of the writer of that work.

Give . . . dogs, from Matt. vii. 6 exactly. The text is
more generally applied in Clem. Alex., *Strom.* ii. 2 [7], and
Tertullian, *de Præscr.* 41. Cf. the use of the "Sancta
Sanctis" in the liturgies.

X. 1. *after ye are filled* (ἐμπλησθῆναι). That this refers
to the eucharist it is difficult to believe; if it refers to the
agape it is quite intelligible. For a Jewish parallel, see
C. Taylor, *Teaching,* p. 130: "The chagigah was eaten first
that the passover might be eaten after being filled." That
it was not a suitable phrase for the eucharist is seen from
the change made by the writer of *Ap. Const.* vii. 26 (who
had transformed the preceding prayer for use by communicants), for he alters it to "after the partaking" (μετάληψιν;
cf. Justin, *Apol.* i. 67: "a partaking of that over which
thanks have been given, μετάληψις ἀπὸ τῶν εὐχαρισθέντων).
Tertullian uses a phrase similar to that of *Did.* in speaking
of the agape and the absence of gluttony at it: "thus they
are satiated" (*ita saturantur, Apol.* 39); so *Eg. Ch. Ord.*:
"taste sufficiently" (*sufficienter gustate,* Connolly, p. 188),

2. We thank thee, Holy Father, for thy holy name, which thou hast made to dwell in our hearts, and for the knowledge, faith, and immortality, which thou didst make known to us through Jesus, thy servant. Glory be to thee for ever. 3. Thou, Almighty Lord, didst create

Test. of our Lord : "let them eat abundantly" (ii. 13). It has been suggested on the other hand that the *Didache* takes its verb from John vi. 12, while the Synoptists use χορτάζομαι (of the Miraculous Feeding). But this, if true, makes it the more probable that the agape is here referred to.

2. It has been suggested that "Holy Father" and "thy name" come from John xvii. 11; but "thy name" and "hast made to dwell" (κατεσκήνωσας) are from Jer. vii. 12 LXX. This verb is more often intransitive "to dwell," *e. g.* Matt. xiii. 32, Clem. Rom., *Cor.* 58, and it is taken so in the Vulgate of Jer. vii. 12.—For "made known," see on ix. 3. Our writer could not have got "knowledge" (γνῶσις) or "immortality" (ἀθανασία) from the Johannine writings, for they do not occur there.—For "Jesus thy servant," see on ix. 2.—For "our hearts" the MS by error reads "your hearts"; see on iv. 11, xiv. 1.

3. *Almighty Lord* (δέσποτα). For the substantive (lit. "Master") see Luke ii. 29, Acts iv. 24, 2 Pet. ii. 1, Jude 4, Rev. vi. 10, Clem. Rom. vii. 5 (where compare Lightfoot's note; it is often applied to the Father in Clement). In 2 Peter and Jude it is used of our Lord, and possibly in Revelation.—The complete phrase is often found in the liturgies (*Ap. Const.* vii. 25, viii. 5, Brightman, pp. 41, 133).

spiritual meat . . . eternal. This phrase also occurs in *Ap. Ch. Ord.* 12, its only connection with *Did.* outside the *Two Ways*, and is inserted in *Ap. Ch. Ord.* in the passage about remembering the preacher (*Did.* iv. 1 f., *q.v.*). This seems conclusive as to the priority of *Did.*, if there is any direct obligation on either side. Our author could not possibly have taken the phrase from *Ap. Ch. Ord.* out of its context, and put it in a prayer at a later stage of the book. Probably, on the other hand, *Ap. Ch. Ord.* did not get the phrase from *Did.*, but it was a common one in early

THE DIDACHE

all things for thy name's sake, and gavest meat and drink for men to enjoy, that they might give thanks unto thee, and to us didst vouchsafe spiritual meat and drink and life eternal, through thy servant. 4. Above all we thank thee because thou art mighty. Glory be to thee for ever. 5. Remember, Lord, thy Church, to deliver her from all evil, and to perfect her in thy love, and gather together from the four winds her that is sanctified into thy kingdom which thou didst prepare for her. For thine is the power and the glory for ever. 6. Come grace,

Christian liturgical language. The *Didache* prayers may not have been original in that writer.—This phrase is the nearest approach in our author to the idea of sacramental grace; though some think that it refers to the *teaching* of our Lord.

4. The MS by error omits " to thee."

5. *evil.* See above on viii. 2. For " perfect . . . love " see 1 John iv. 18; "*gather* . . . *winds* " is from Matt. xxiv. 31; " thy kingdom . . . for her " is from Matt. xxv. 34.

6. *Hosanna to the God of David.* In the parallel *Ap. Const.* vii. 26 " Son of David," and so Matt. xxi. 9 (see Mark xi. 10, which, however, omits " Son " and refers to the " kingdom " of David : cf. John xii. 13). It is doubtful whether *Did.* applies the phrase to our Lord, or to the Father. The liturgies have " Hosanna to the Son of David " before communion (*Ap. Const.* viii. 13), or " Hosanna in the highest " at the Sanctus (Brightman, 51, 86), but this feature is absent from many of them. Here, in *Did.*, it probably comes before communion (see on ix. 1).

let him come. These words would be out of place after reception of Holy Communion. This " fencing of the tables " appears in almost all the liturgies, and occurs before the Offertory. An early specimen (*c.* A.D. 350) is that in the *Test. of our Lord*, where the deacon says to the people : " If any man have wrath against his companion, let him be

and let this world pass away. Hosanna to the God of David. If any is holy, let him come:

reconciled; if any man have a conscience without faith, let him confess; if any man have a thought foreign to the commandments, let him depart; if any man have fallen into sin, let him not hide himself; . . . if any man be a stranger to the commandments of Jesus, let him depart; if any man despise the prophets, let him separate himself," etc. (i. 23). See also *Ap. Const.* viii. 12, the dismissal of catechumens and penitents having already taken place. The *Didache* and the parallel *Ap. Const.* vii. 26, do not say that the unholy are to *depart*, but this is probably the meaning. In *Eg. Ch. Ord.* the liturgy begins at the Offertory, and there is no parallel to this.

Maranatha, from 1 Cor. xvi. 22, used here as an eucharistic watchword, placed in *Ap. Const.* vii. 26 before the Hosanna. This Aramaic expression (it is two words), which should be divided by a full-stop from the preceding "Anathema" in 1 Cor. (see R.V.) is of doubtful meaning. It has been rendered "The Lord hath come," or "Our Lord hath come," or "Our Lord cometh" (so R.V. m.), or "Our Lord, come" (cf. Rev. xxii. 20), or "Our Lord is the sign." It must have been a familiar watchword in St Paul's time, for he gives it in Aramaic.

Amen. Cf. 1 Cor. xiv. 16. The *Didache* does not give it at the end of the prayers, though it would be unsafe to affirm that it is meant to be used here *only*. Justin describes the people's Amen after the eucharistic "prayers and thanksgivings" (*Apol.* i. 65, 67). One of the most characteristic uses of Amen was by the communicant after reception: *Eg. Ch. Ord.* (Connolly, p. 186); Eusebius, *H.E.* vi. 43 (Roman usage); *Test. of our Lord* (ii. 10); *Can. of Hippol.* (can. xix, ed. Achelis § 147); *Ap. Const.* viii. 13; and in the developed liturgies (Brightman, pp. 186, 241, etc.). To this last Amen Tertullian seems to refer (*de Spect.* 25) : "ex ore quo Amen in sanctum protuleris," *i. e.* over the consecrated elements. So in the *Ambrosian Liturgy* (C. E. Hammond, *Lit. E. and W.*, Oxford, 1878, p. 354).—The absence of a detailed description of the eucharist may be due to reserve about sacred things.

XI] THE DIDACHE 33

if any is unholy let him repent. Maranatha.
Amen. 7. But suffer the prophets to give
thanks as much as they will.

CHAPTER XI

1. Whosoever then shall come and teach you
all these things aforesaid, receive him. 2. But

7. *the prophets.* See ch. xi. The parallel *Ap. Const.*
vii. 26, has : " But suffer your *presbyters* to give thanks "
(εὐχαριστεῖν, so *Did.*), thus omitting the reference to extemporaneous prayer. Dr. J. A. Robinson thinks that the
Did. writer here interprets 1 Cor. xiv. 16 as meaning that a
prophet blessed in the Spirit.—It is probable that at first
the prayers were mostly extemporaneous, though guided by
some fixed scheme. Thus in Justin Martyr the " president "
(προεστώς) " offers thanks at considerable length . . . according to his ability " (*Apol.* i. 65, 67). The *Didache* gives
special latitude to the itinerant ministry, but it is not said
that any Christian might ordinarily preside at the eucharist;
on the contrary (xv. 11, *q.v.*) clergy are provided for this very
purpose. In Clement of Rome (*Cor.* 41) each Christian is to
take his proper place in the thanksgiving or eucharist of the
Church (see Lightfoot's note); and the significant words are
added: " not transgressing the appointed rule of his
ministry " (λειτουργίας). Traces of this liberty of improvisation are found in the Roman liturgy as late as the
sixth century, as seen in the *Leonine Sacramentary*
(L. Duchesne, *Christian Worship*, Eng. tr., London, 1903,
p. 179).—After this section *Ap. Const.* vii. 27 interpolates
a thanksgiving over the " unguent " (μύρον), with the short
doxology, " for thine is the glory and the power for ever,
Amen."

The itinerant ministry.—XI. 1. This ministry consists of
" apostles, prophets, and teachers "; cf. 1 Cor. xii. 28. It
has been suggested that here three different grades of itinerants are meant; and, if so, the " apostles " of the *Didache*
are rightly adjudged to be " shadowy "; nothing is said
about them after xi. 6, and no functions are assigned to

if the teacher himself turn and teach another doctrine to pervert, hear him not. But unto the increase of righteousness and of the knowledge of the Lord, receive him as the Lord 3. And

them. But are they not the same persons as the prophets, though under a different aspect? As bearing a message these itinerants are apostles; as prophesying they are prophets. In xi. 3 they are grouped under one article (τῶν ἀποστόλων καὶ προφητῶν) as in Eph. ii. 25, where Dr F. J. A. Hort (*Christian Ecclesia*, p. 165) thinks that the same persons are meant (not in Eph. iv. 11). It may be answered that the "teacher" is not the same as the "prophet" in *Did.* xiii. 1 f. But the cases are not parallel. In xi. 10 f. the prophet teaches, and in xv. 1 f. "the prophets and teachers" are apparently identical and are twice joined under one article (τῶν προφητῶν καὶ διδασκάλων); while in xiii. 1 f. the prophet is the itinerant official, and the "true teacher" is any one who has a "word of exhortation" (Acts xiii. 15), whether he be an official or not, and whether he be a local man or come from the outside. Thus xiii. 2 is a parenthesis, giving the general principle that a true teacher is worthy of maintenance. We may remember that Origen, while still a layman, was yet a teacher. —Almost the whole of this chapter is omitted in *Ap. Const.* vii, as being anachronistic in the fourth century; instead we have a short section about a stranger : "if he teach another doctrine " (so *Did.*) he is not to be allowed to "give thanks."

3. *apostles*. For the fluidity of phraseology with regard to the Christian Ministry in the New Testament, see article "Ministry (early Christian)" in Hastings' *Encycl. of Religion and Ethics* viii. 662a. The name "apostles" is not confined to the Twelve; see Lightfoot, Appended Note in his *Comm. on Galatians*, p. 92 (ed. 6). It may even be used in the N.T. of Andronicus, Junias, Silvanus, and others (Rom. xvi. 7, 1 Thess. ii. 6); it means a "missionary delegate" (2 Cor. viii. 23, Phil. ii. 25). In Syriac it is constantly used of any missionary, *e. g.* of Addai and Mari.

the decree of the gospel, perhaps referring to Matt. x. 5 ff.; but these instructions were not intended to be observed after the Resurrection.

XI] THE DIDACHE 35

as touching the apostles and prophets, according to the decree of the gospel, so do ye. 4. But let every apostle that cometh unto you be received as the Lord. 5. And he shall stay one day, and, if need be, the next also, but, if he stay three, he is a false prophet. 6. And, when the apostle goeth forth, let him take nothing save bread, till he reach his lodging, but if he ask money, he is a false prophet. 7. And every prophet that

5. *he shall stay.* The MS inserts "not." Perhaps εἰ μή has dropped out (Harnack, Lightfoot), and the meaning is "he shall not stay more than one day."

7. *speaketh in the Spirit.* In Jewish, and presumably in Christian, prophecy, the Spirit speaks through the prophet, but the prophet never impersonates the Spirit as Simon Magus did (Acts viii. 9 f.), and also Montanus, who claimed to be God come down in man. It was this "possession," involving the claim to speak infallibly on all topics, and even to override other prophets, that the Church resisted in the Montanists (Eusebius, *H.E.* v. 16 f.). The vital question was whether prophets lost their self-command when prophesying, and on this the *Didache* is silent. See G. Salmon, *Dict. Chr. Biog.* iv. 808*b*, and article "Montanus" in iii. 935; also Gore-Turner, *Church and the Ministry*, Notes H, I.— Prophecy continued in the Church long after apostolic times. Justin (*Dial.* 82) says: "The prophetic gifts remain with us." Irenæus (*Haer.* V vi. 2) says that he had heard of many brethren in the Church who possessed prophetic gifts. Hermas and others were prophets. In *Ap. Ch. Ord.* 21, two of the widows are to expect revelations. But in the *Didache* there are no prophetesses, as in Montanism; and the prophet is an official person.

ye shall not try nor judge. In the subsequent sections the prophet is to be judged by his "manners" or life. Dr. Salmon suggests (*Dict. Chr. Biog.* iv. 808*b*) that what is meant here is that the prophets are not to be tested by exorcism, as was attempted in the case of Montanist prophetesses, with the result of a great outcry.—The words speaketh in the Spirit ye shall not try nor judge : for every sin shall be forgiven, but this sin shall not be forgiven. 8. But not every one that speaketh in the Spirit is a prophet, but if he have the manners of the Lord. By their manners then shall the false prophet and the prophet be known. 9. And no prophet that † ordereth † a table in the Spirit shall eat of it, else is he a false prophet. 10. And every prophet that teacheth the truth if he doeth not what he teacheth, is a false prophet. 11. But every approved true prophet, who † doeth for an earthly mystery of the Church, † but teacheth not others to do what he himself doeth, shall not be judged among you, for he hath his judgment with God : for even so did the ancient prophets also. 12. But whosoever shall say in the Spirit : Give me money, or any

which follow are an adaptation of Matt. xii. 31. The testing in the *Didache* is a moral one, that in 1 John iv. 1–3 a doctrinal one; the *Didache* rather follows Matt. vii. 15–20.

9. *ordereth* (ὁρίζων). The MS has ὁ ῥίζων, clearly in error. This is certainly an agape, given at the command of a prophet, who is not to impose on the charity of the people.

11. *who doeth . . . Church* (ποιῶν εἰς μυστήριον κοσμικὸν ἐκκλησίας). Lightfoot renders : "if he doeth ought as an outward mystery typical of the Church," but the text is probably corrupt, and if so we cannot guess at the meaning of the first two clauses. But if the prophet is "approved" and "true" (as is shown by his life), he is not to be judged any more than the "ancient prophets." These last are probably the Old Testament prophets, though possibly the first Christian prophets may be intended (Harnack).

12. *Give me money*. The prophet might take money (xiii. 7), but he might not ask for it, except on behalf of the poor.

XII] THE DIDACHE 37

other thing, ye shall not hearken to him: but, if he bid you give for others that are in need, let no man judge him.

CHAPTER XII

1. Let every one that cometh in the name of the Lord be received, and then, when ye have proved him, ye shall know, for ye shall have understanding [to distinguish] between the right hand and the left. 2. If he that cometh is a passer-by, succour him as far as ye can; but he shall not abide with you longer than two or three days unless there be necessity. 3. But if he be minded to settle among you, and be a craftsman, let him work and eat. 4. But, if he hath no trade, according to your understanding provide

XII. Of this chapter *Ap. Const.* vii. 28 retains only the first section, altered.

1. *that cometh . . . Lord.* Cf. Matt. xxi. 9 (from Ps. cxvii. 26). Κύριος without the article, as here, is constantly used for Yahweh, *e.g.* thirty times in St Luke.

to distinguish, not in the MS, which has "ye shall have understanding on the right hand and on the left" (Lightfoot). The *Ap. Const.* vii. 28 has, "ye have understanding and are able to know the right hand and the left, and to distinguish false teachers from (true) teachers." In both cases the reference is to Jonah iv. 11 LXX (οἵτινες οὐκ ἔγνωσαν δεξιὰν αὐτῶν ἢ ἀριστερὰν αὐτῶν).

2. *a passer by* (πάροδιος), usually meaning "on the road."

unless. The MS has ἐάν "if" only, but the sense requires the insertion of μή "not."

3. *work and eat.* Cf. 2 Thess. iii. 10.

that he shall not live idle among you, being a Christian. 5. But, if he will not do this, he is a Christmonger: of such men beware.

CHAPTER XIII

1. But every true prophet, who is minded to settle among you, is worthy of his maintenance. 2. In like manner a true teacher also is worthy, like every workman, of his maintenance. 3. Thou

5. *Christmonger* (χριστέμπορος), " one who makes merchandise of Christ " as opposed to a " Christian " (§ 4). This word is found often in the fourth century. Basil, *Ep.* ccxl. 3: " these are Christmongers and not Christians "; Pseudo-Ignatius, *Trall.* 6: " not Christians but Christmongers "; but the word is absent from the *Ap. Const.* vii. 28 (parallel to *Did.*). It is also found in Pseudo-Ignatius, *Magn.* 9, Gregory of Nazianzus, *Orat.* xl. 11, and Athanasius, *in Matt.* vii. 15 (i. 1026); and χριστεμπορία is found in Alexander of Alexandria's letter to Alexander of Constantinople (early fourth century; Theodoret, *H.E.* i. 3). For its bearing on the date of the *Didache*, see Introd., § 6.

XIII. 1. The *Ap. Const.* vii. 28 has this, adding " or teacher "; for " who is minded to settle among you " it has " coming to you," an itinerant ministry being anachronistic in the fourth century; and it condenses our § 2 by adding to § 1, " as a workman of the word of righteousness."—The quotation is from Matt. x. 10, which has also " the workman " as our § 2. The parallel Luke x. 7 has " hire " for " maintenance," or " food " (τροφή) of Matt. and *Did.*

2. *teacher.* See on xi. 1. " Every " is not in our MS.

3. *first-fruits.* In *Ap. Const.* vii. 29 they are given to the priests (ἱερεῦσιν), tithes to the orphan, widow, poor, and proselyte. Payment is almost entirely in kind. Under the Empire high officials on service in the provinces received a great part of their appointments in articles of use (*Hist. Aug.,*

shalt take therefore all first-fruits of the produce of winepress and threshing floor, of oxen and sheep, and give them to the prophets; for they are your high priests. 4. But if ye have no prophet, give to the poor. 5. If thou art making bread, take the first-fruits and give according to the commandment. 6. In like manner, when thou openest a jar of wine or oil, take the first-fruits and give to the prophets. 7. And of money, and raiment, and of every chattel, take the first-fruits, as seemeth thee good, and give according to the commandment.

Claudius, xiv.). A rustic community is contemplated in the *Didache*.

give them. The MS has, by repetition, "give the first-fruits."

for they are your high priests (ἀρχιερεῖς). The passage is adapted from Numb. xviii. 12 ff., Deut. xviii. 3 f., where the first-fruits are given to Aaron and his sons and daughters (Deut., " the priests, the Levites "). This is the significance of " *your* (Christian) high priests " (the pronoun is emphatic). There is no evidence here or elsewhere that prophets were ordinarily called " high priests." In the strictest sense Christ is the only high priest; but in Christian antiquity the diocesan bishop was, in a lower sense, so called, as in Tertullian (*de Bapt.* 17, " summus sacerdos qui est episcopus "); Hippolytus (*Ref.* i, Introd., ἀρχιερατεία); *Eg. Ch. Ord.* (Connolly, p. 175); the *Older Didascalia* (Funk, i. 102, Hauler, p. 36 f., etc.); *Canons of Hippolytus* (can. xxiv, ed. Achelis § 200) ; *Test. of our Lord* (ii. 21); and often in *Ap. Const.*—With the *Did.* phrase cf. Justin, *Dial.* 116: " We are the true high-priestly (ἀρχιερατικόν) race of God."

5. *bread* (σιτίαν), in *Ap. Const.* vii. 29 "warm loaves" (ἄρτων θερμῶν); perhaps the writer did not know the *Did.* word, which is very rare as a feminine. This section seems to come from Numb. xv. 20–22 (note " all these commandments "); cf. Neh. x. 37.

CHAPTER XIV

1. And on the Lord's day of the Lord come together and break bread and give thanks, having † first † confessed your transgressions, that our sacrifice may be pure. 2. But whoso hath a dispute with his fellow, let him not come together with you, until they be reconciled, that our sacrifice be not polluted. 3. For this is that

The Sunday Service.—XIV. 1. Sunday is the only day here mentioned for the eucharist and for public service (cf. Acts xx. 7), and in the earliest ages this was the custom. So the *Older Didascalia* (Funk, i. 170—the parallel *Ap. Const.* substitutes daily services); *Ap. Ch. Ord.* 19; Justin (*Apol.* i. 67), etc. But even in Tertullian's time a more frequent use of the eucharist was beginning in "Africa" (*de Orat.* 19). See further the present editor's *Ancient Church Orders*, pp. 55-59. In particular, Saturdays became a common day for the eucharist in the East. In *Ap. Const.* vii. 23 (parallel to *Did.* viii.) Saturday and Sunday are both feasts.

the Lord's day of the Lord (κυριακὴν κυρίου), a curious pleonasm. For κυριακή see Rev. i. 10, Ignatius, *Magn.* ix.; Melito of Sardis (c. A.D. 190) wrote a treatise περὶ κυριακῆς (Eusebius, *H.E.* iv. 26). The phrase in *Did.* shows that ἡ κυριακή was not then a well-established name.

first. The MS has προσεξομολογησάμενοι, probably in error for προεξ.

our sacrifice, so the MS, which has "your sacrifice" in § 2, and "your" is probably right here also; ἡμῶν and ὑμῶν are frequently interchanged by the scribes, owing to their being pronounced alike in late Greek. See on iv. 11, x. 2.

2. *dispute* (ἀμφιβολίαν), lit. "an attack on both sides."

3. This is loosely cited from Mal. i. 11 LXX, a passage often quoted with reference to the eucharist, as in Justin, *Dial.* 28, 41, 116; Irenæus, *Haer.* IV xvii. 5, xviii. 1; Tertullian, *adv. Jud.* 5, *adv. Marc.* iii. 22; Clem. Alex., *Strom.* v. 14 [136].

THE DIDACHE

which was spoken of by the Lord: In every place and time offer me a pure sacrifice; for I am a great King, saith the Lord, and my name is wonderful among the Gentiles.

CHAPTER XV

1. Elect therefore for yourselves bishops and deacons worthy of the Lord, men meek and not covetous, and true and approved: for they also minister unto you the ministry of the prophets

The local ministry.—XV. 1. This consists of "bishops" and "deacons," just as in the New Testament, and in Clement of Rome (*Cor.* 42), where the apostles are said to have preached everywhere in (κατά) countries and cities and appointed their first-fruits . . . to be bishops and deacons unto them that believe. These "bishops" in the N.T. are the same as "presbyters"—in Acts xx. 17, 28, the same persons are called by both titles, and 1 Tim. iii. 1–7 describes the qualifications of "bishops," while 1 Tim. v. 17–19 gives regulations for "presbyters" as for those who have already been mentioned in the Epistle; cf. Tit. i. 5, 7: "appoint presbyters in every city . . . for the bishop must be blameless." [Dr. Hort's view (*Christian Ecclesia*, pp. 98 f., 189 ff.) that "bishops" and "deacons" are non-technical descriptions in the N.T., of "those who have oversight" and "those who minister," is scarcely probable.] In Clement also (*Cor.* 44) "presbyters" are mentioned as those already spoken of, and their "episcopate" (ἐπισκοπή). In the *Didache*, however, the name "presbyter" is not found. The writer, who at least had read Acts (Introd., § 5), must have known the name, but probably in his community it was not used. It is possible that, where both names were used, "presbyter" expressed the rank, "bishop" the function.

and teachers. 2. Therefore despise them not:
for these are they which are honoured of you

The identity in the N.T. of " bishops " and " presbyters "
was completely forgotten by the end of the second century.
Irenæus (*Haer.* III xiv. 2), referring to Acts xx. 17 ff., speaks
of St Paul meeting at Miletus bishops and presbyters from
Ephesus *and the other cities,* these words being added because
of the plural " bishops," whom Irenæus took to be bishops
in the later sense (see further, Hastings, *Encycl. of Rel. and
Eth.* viii. 660). This is a great argument for the early date
of the *Didache*, and it is much against Dr. Robinson's view
(Introd., § 7) that the writer was describing an imaginary state
of things as drawn from his knowledge of the N.T.; for he
must there have read of presbyters, and why should he,
on Dr. Robinson's hypothesis, have omitted them? The
parallel *Ap. Const.* vii. 31 has " bishops, presbyters, and
deacons," taking " bishops " in the later sense.

Elect. Rather " appoint," χειροτονήσατε, a general word
including the whole process of choosing and appointing
ministers. It neither affirms nor negatives the laying on
of hands, though it was often used for " ordain." The
Ap. Const. have here προχειρίσασθε " elect," " choose "; probably χειροτονεῖν in the fourth century would have suggested
that the whole congregation ordained. For the election of
the clergy by the laity see Hastings, *Enc. Rel. Eth.* vii. 768.

therefore. The principal object of the local ministry is
that the eucharist on the Lord's day may be celebrated.
Thus the right of celebrating the eucharist appears to be
restricted in *Did.* to the clergy, and we cannot draw the
inference from x. 7 that if a prophet was not present any
Christian might preside.

they also minister . . . teachers. The ministry (λειτουργία)
of the settled pastor is one with that of the itinerant. To
use a modern phrase, the one is as " charismatic " as the
other. Perhaps we have here a reminiscence of the prophets
and teachers " ministering " (λειτουργούντων) in Acts xiii.
1 f. On the question of the identity of the prophets and
teachers, see on xi. 1.

2. *despise them not.* The local ministry has not yet arrived
at the paramount position which it soon attained.

XVI] THE DIDACHE 43

with the prophets and teachers. 3. And reprove one another, not in wrath but in peace, as ye have it in the gospel: and to him that behaveth amiss against another let no man speak, neither let him hear a word from you, until he repent. 4. But your prayers and alms and all that ye do, do so as ye have it in the gospel of our Lord.

CHAPTER XVI

1. Watch over your life: let not your lamps be extinguished, neither let your loins be ungirt, but be ye ready: for ye know not the hour in which our Lord doth come. 2. But ye shall be frequently gathered together, seeking the things that belong unto your souls. For the whole

3. *behaveth amiss* (ἀστοχοῦντι); lit. "to miss the mark." Cf. Ecclus. vii. 6, viii. 9, 1 Tim. i. 6, vi. 21, 2 Tim. ii. 18.

Apocalyptic epilogue.—XVI. 1. Reminiscence of Matt. xxv. 1, Luke xii. 35 (but the "ungirt," ἐκλυέσθωσαν, is not from St Luke's "girded," περιεζωσμένοι), Matt. xxiv. 44; for "our Lord," Matt. has "the Son of Man."

2. *belong unto* (ἀνήκοντα), or "are fitting for" (Lightfoot).

For the whole time . . . profit you. Barnabas (§ 4) has "For the whole time of our faith shall profit us nothing, except now in the lawless time and the coming stumbling-blocks we resist, as becometh sons of God, that the Black One [see on *Did.* v. 1] may not effect an entrance." In Barnabas the present time and the immediate future are in view, in the *Didache* "the last time." There is probably here no literary obligation on either side, but the first few words would seem to have been a proverbial saying. The parallel *Ap. Const.* vii. 31 has: "Your former good deeds shall not benefit (ὀνήσει for *Did.* ὠφελήσει) if at your last ye go astray from the true faith."

F

time of your faith shall not profit you, except ye be perfected in the last time. 3. For in the last days false prophets and corrupters shall abound, and the sheep shall be turned into wolves, and love shall be turned into hate. 4. For, as lawlessness increaseth, they shall hate and persecute and deliver up one another; and then shall appear the World-deceiver as son of God, and shall do signs and wonders, and the earth shall be delivered up into his hands, and he shall commit iniquities which have never been seen from the beginning. 5. Then shall the race of man come into the fiery trial of testing, and many shall be offended and perish, but they who

3. *false prophets, wolves*, a reminiscence of Matt. vii. 15. Our author lays stress on the persecution of Christians by Christians (Introd., § 6).

4. Reminiscence of Matt. xxiv. 10, 30, 24, Luke xxi. 10, woven together; the "lawlessness" is perhaps from 2 Thess. . 7, and the "World-deceiver" (κοσμοπλανής or κοσμοπλάνος, a late word) resembles the "Man of Sin," the "lawless one" of 2 Thess. ii. 3, 8. The *Ap. Const.* explicitly quotes that last verse. In Rev. xii. 9 the "deceiver of the whole world" is ὁ πλανῶν τὴν οἰκουμένην ὅλην.

as son (υἱός) *of God*, that is, as Antichrist.

5. *the race* (κτίσις). Harnack conjectures κρίσις "judgment."

fiery trial (πύρωσις). For the word cf. 1 Pet. iv. 12.

they who endure . . . saved. From Matt. x. 22, xxiv. 13.

the Curse (κατάθεμα, for κατανάθεμα). *Ap. Const.* omits this. The word (not a classical one) occurs in Rev. xxii. 3, but not of our Lord (see Swete's note there); it is stronger than ἀνάθεμα. It may mean "by him whom men curse" (1 Cor. xii. 3) or "by him who became a curse for us" (Gal. iii. 13, where κατάρα is used, not κατάθεμα. Harnack unnecessarily reads ἀπό ("saved from") for ὑπό ("by").

XVI] THE DIDACHE 45

endure in their faith shall be saved by the Curse himself. 6. And then shall appear the signs of the truth : first a sign of spreading out in heaven, then a sign of the sound of a trumpet, and the third the resurrection of the dead. 7. But not

6. *a sign of spreading out* (ἐκπετάσεως) *in heaven.* No satisfactory explanation has been given of this obscure expression, and the author of *Ap. Const.* could not have understood it, for he alters it to "the sign of the Son of man in heaven" (vii. 32), from Matt. xxiv. 30, which is doubtless the source of the *Did.* phrase, and which refers to the Second Advent. Dr Salmon (*Introd. to the N.T.* xxvi, ed. 6, p. 562) and others suggest that we have here a quotation from Barnabas (§ 12), who interprets Isa. lxv. 2 : " I have stretched forth (ἐξεπέτασα) my hands to a disobedient and gainsaying people," of our Lord's stretching forth his hands on the cross, and Justin (*Apol.* i. 35, cf. *Dial.* 114) and other Fathers have the same exegesis (cf. also Rom. x. 21). With this cf. *Test. of our Lord,* i. 23: "he stretched forth his hands to suffering," a phrase denoting the voluntary nature of the Passion; *Eg. Ch. Ord.* (Connolly, p. 176, Brightman, *Lit. E. and W.,* p. 190): "that he might fulfil thy will . . . by stretching out his hands . . . who was delivered of his own will to the passion " (cf. *Abyssinian Liturgy,* Brightman, p. 232). But this hardly suits the *Didache* passage; our author would not have used his short expression without explanation if this was his meaning; moreover, if this interpretation is correct we have here the one allusion in the book to any event in our Lord's earthly life, and this fact weighs heavily against it. In any case there is no need to postulate a quotation from Barnabas. The reference in *Did.* is to something that will happen at the Last Day, and appears rather to be to the fact that our Lord will be manifested to all in every part of the world : every eye shall see him (Rev. i. 7).

the sound of a trumpet, from Matt. xxiv. 31; cf. 1 Cor. xv. 52, 1 Thess. iv. 16.

7. *not of all.* The "resurrection of the dead" (ἀνάστασις νεκρῶν, cf. Acts xxiv. 21, 1 Cor. xv. 13) is therefore the

of all, but as it was said : The Lord shall come
and all the saints with him. 8. Then shall the
world behold the Lord coming on the clouds of
heaven.

resurrection of the just; cf. Phil. iii. 11. Nothing is said
here of the resurrection of the unjust (John v. 28 f., Acts
xxiv. 15) "to shame and everlasting contempt" (Dan.
xii. 2).

as it was said. The quotation is from Zech. xiv. 5 LXX,
where we read, "the Lord my God" (Κύριος ὁ θεός μου) for
ὁ Κύριος of *Did.* The Zechariah passage is paraphrased in
1 Thess. iii. 13, "the coming of our Lord Jesus with all his
saints" (see G. Milligan's note). The "saints" or "holy
ones" (οἱ ἅγιοι) in *Did.* must include the angels, as they are
certainly included in Zechariah; but angels are not elsewhere
referred to by our author.—The *Ap. Const.* vii. 32 adds, "in
a whirlwind" (or "earthquake," συσσεισμῷ).— Our author
is not a professed Chiliast; there is no hint of a millennium,
which he neither denies nor asserts (see Introd., § 6).

8. From Matt. xxiv. 30, with the addition of "the world"
and the substitution of "the Lord" for "the Son of Man."
The use of "the Lord" absolutely, in narrative, with reference to Jesus, is found only in St Luke of the Synoptists.
Our author omits "with power and great glory" of Matt.

The *Didache* here ends abruptly, perhaps in the middle o
a sentence; the parallel *Ap. Const.* vii. 32 (which omits our
§ 8, except that it adds "on the clouds" to our § 7) goes on
without a break to "with the angels of his power on the
throne of the kingdom, to condemn the World-deceiver,
(the) Devil, and to render to each one according to his deeds"
(πρᾶξιν), and adds a section about the punishment of the
wicked and the reward of the righteous. It may be suspected
that there was originally something of this in the *Didache,*
and that the archetype of our manuscript had lost its last
leaf.

INDEX

A

Abyssinian Liturgy, 45
Addai, 34
Agape, xx, xxv, xxviii, 24 f., 28 f., 36
Aleatoribus, de, xviii
Alexander of Alexandria, 38
Alexandrinisms, xxix
Ambrosian Liturgy, 32
Amen, 32
Anathema, 32, 44
Angels, xiv, 2, 17, 46
Anointing, absence of, 20
Antichrist, 44
Apocalyptic Epilogue, 43
Apostles, xxxvi f., 33 f.
——in *Ap. Ch. Ord.*, xi, xvi f.
Apostles, Canons of the, xviii, 22
'Apostles' Creed,' the name, xxxiv
Apostolic Church Order, viii–xii, xv, xxiv, xxvii, xxxiiif., xxxvii, 1 f., 4–14, 30, 35, 40
Apostolic Constitutions, viii f., xvii f., xxxiii, xxxvii, 3, 8, 12 f., 15–17, 19–34, 37–40, 42–45
Apostolic fiction, xvi–xix, xxi, xxxii–xxxv
Apostolic Tradition, the, xvii, xxxiii
Appointment of clergy, 41 f.
Asceticism, 17 f.
Astrologers, 8

'Athanasian Creed,' the name, xxxiv
Athanasius, xviii, xxxiv, 28, 38
Athenagoras, 18
Atonement and redemption, xix, 2, 28
Augurs, 7
Augustine, 8

B

Baptism, xx, 18–21
——by affusion, xxix f., 20
——, fasting before, 21
——into the Name of the Lord, 29
Barnabas, Epistle of, viii–xv, xxii, xxvi, 1 f., 4–7, 9–16, 26, 43, 45
Basil, 38
Bibliography, xxxvii f.
Bishops, xxxvi, 39, 41 f.
Black One, the, 15, 43
Bread, breaking of, 26–28

C

Canons of Hippolytus, xxxiii, 8, 19, 21 f., 29, 32, 39
Cassiodorus, 5
Catechumens, 21, 28, 32
Celsus, 26
Charismatic ministry, xxxi, 42
Chiliasm, xxviii f., 46
'Christmonger,' xxx, 38
'Church,' xxviii, 15

INDEX

Circumcision, xx
Clement of Alexandria, x, xxii–xxiv, xxvii–xxix, 4, 9, 15, 22, 24, 26 f., 29, 40
Clement of Rome, vii, xvi–xviii, xxiii, xxx, 26, 30, 33, 41
——, Pseudo, vii, xxvii, 18
Clementine Homilies and Recognitions, xxxiv, 19, 21
Codex Bezae, 2
Confession, 15
Cornelius, Pope, 20
Cup in Eucharist or Agape, 25 f.
Curse, the, 44
Cyprian, xxix f., 20, 24, 28
——, Pseudo, xviii

D

Date of *Didache*, xxvi–xxxvii
David, God of, xix, 32
——, Vine of, xxiv, xxix, 26
Deacons, xxxvi, 41
Dead gods, xxvii, 18
Decalogue, ix, xii, 5 f.
Diatessaron, xxv f.
Didascalia, Older, xviii, xxv f., xxvii, xxxiii, 3, 22, 39 f.
——, Arabic, 22
Diocesan Episcopacy, xxxvi
Diognetus, Epistle to, 18
Disciplina arcani, xxx, 32
Divinity of our Lord, xix, xxix, 31
Doxologies, xxv, xxxvii, 23, 33
Duae Viae, xix. See *Two Ways*.

E

Easter and Lent not mentioned, xxvi, 22
Edessene Canons, xviii, 22
Egypt, xxxvii
Egyptian Church Order, vi, xvii, xxv, xxviii, xxxiii, 8, 17, 19, 21, 23, 25, 28 f., 32, 39, 45

Enoch, books of, xxxiii f.
Epiphanius, 22
Epitome of *Apost. Const.*, xviif.
Eucharist, xx, 24 f., 31 f., 40, 42
Eusebius, xviii, 20, 35, 40
Evil One, the, xxvii, 23, 31
Exomologesis, 15
Exorcism, 35
Extempore prayer, 24, 33

F

Fast before baptism, 21
——, Wed. and Fri., xxviii, 3, 22
Fasting, xxv f., 3, 22 f.
'Fencing the tables,' 24, 27 f., 31 f.
First-fruits, 38 f.

G

Gentiles, xvii, xx, 1, 3, 18
Golden Rule, the, xx, 2
'Gospel, the,' ('his'), xxvii, 23
Gregory of Nazianzus, 38
Gregory of Nyssa, 23

H

Hadrian, 8
Hermas, xxii–xxiv, xxvi f., xxxvi, 4, 22, 35
High-priests, 39
Hippolytus, vi, xvii f., xxviii, xxxiii f., 8, 17, 39. See *Canons*, and *Egyptian Church Order*.
Hippolytus, Constitutions through, see Epitome
Holy Spirit, the, xix, 35
Hosanna, xx, 31
Hours of prayer, xxviii, 24
Humanity of our Lord, xxix
'Hypocrites' (the Jews), 22

I

Ignatius, xxx, 14, 23, 25, 40
——, Pseudo, 22, 38

INDEX

Immersion, trine, 20
Incarnation, the, xix
Inspiration of prophets, 35
Irenæus, xxviii, 20, 35, 40, 42

J

Jewish character of instruction, xix f.
John, St, little influence on *Didache*, xix, xxxv
Judicium secundum Petrum, xix
Justin Martyr, 21, 29, 32 f., 35, 39 f., 45

L

Lactantius, xvi
Laity, 19, 33, 42
Laodicea, council of, 20
Latin Version of *Two Ways*, xxxviii, 2, 15, 17
Legalistic tone, xx, xxxii
Leon the Notary, vii
Leonine Sacramentary, 33
Libanius, 26
Liberalized Judaism, xx
Life and knowledge, xxix, 27
Line (the book measure), xix
Living water, 19 f.
Lord's day, 40
Lord's prayer, xx, xxvii, 23 f.
Lordship, 12

M

Magic, 7 f.
Maranatha, xx, 27, 32 f.
Mari, 34
Martyrdom of Polycarp, 26
Mathematician, 8
Mediation, xix, 28
Melito, xxvii, 18, 40
Ministry, itinerant, xxxvi, 33-36, 38, 42
———, local, 41 f.
Montanism, xxxi, xxxvi, 35
Mountains, xxxvii, 27 f.
Muratorian Fragment, xxiii f.

N

Neocæsarea, council of, 20
New Testament and *Didache*, xx–xxii, xxxi f., xxxv
Nicephorus, xix
'Night and day,' 11

O

One bread, 27 f.
Origen, x, xxiv, xxix, 10, 22, 26, 34
Oxyrhynchus Logia, 23

P

Palestine, xxxvii
Papias, xxviii
Paul, St, little influence on *Didache*, xix, xxxv
Persecution, xxviii, 44
Peter of Alexandria, 22
Phalaris, Pseudo, xxx
Philo, 8
Pius, xxiv
Place of writing, xxxvii
Plutarch, 8
Porphyry, 8
Presbyters, 41 f.
Prophetesses, xxxvi, 35
Prophets, xxxvi, 24, 32-39
'Purifier,' 8

Q

Quartodecimans, xxv f.

R

Reserve, see Disciplina arcani
Resurrection, the, 28, 45 f.
Roman Liturgy, 33
Rufinus, xviii, 22

S

Sacraments, xix, 31
Sacrifice, the Christian, xx, 40 f.
Sancta Sanctis, 29
Sarapion, xxvi, xxix, 27

INDEX

Saturday Eucharists, 40
Seal, the, 11
Sea water, 19 f.
Septuagint, xxvii
Sermon on the Mount, ix f., 2
' Servant ' (our Lord), 26, 30
Simon Magus, 35
Socrates (historian), 26
Station, 22
Sunday Service, 40
Syria, xxxvii

T

Tatian, xxv f.
Teachers, 33 f., 38
Tertullian, xxviii, 19, 21 f., 24, 29, 32, 39 f.
Testament of our Lord, xvi, xxxiii, 8, 17, 19, 21 f., 27 f., 30–32, 39, 45
Testament of Twelve Patriarchs, xvi, xxxiv
Testing prophets, 35 f.
Theodoret, xxv, 38
Title of *Didache*, xvi–xix, xxxiii, 1
Trinitarian doctrine, xix, 19
Two Ways, viii–xvi, xix, xxi f., xxiv, xxvii, xxxii, xxxvii f., 1–6, 9, 11, 13, 16 f., 19, 30

V

Vine, see David.
Virginitate, de, xxvi, xxix, 28

W

Way of life and death, viii–x, xv f., 1, 13–15, 17
Way of light and darkness, x, xv, 2, 14, 17
' Way,' the, 1 f.
Women not mentioned, xx
' World-deceiver,' 44, 46

Z

Zeus, tomb of, 18

δεσπότης, 30
εἶδος, 7
εἰρηνεύω, 12
ἐκπέτασις, 45
κατάθεμα, 44
κλάσμα, 26 f.
κοσμοπλανής, 44
κύριος, anarthrous, 11, 37, 40, 46
σιτία, 39
στίχος, xix
χριστέμπορος, xxx, 38
χριστόνομος, xxx
χριστοφόρος, xxx
χριστομαθία, xxx

www.ingramcontent.com/pod-product-compliance
Lightning Source LLC
Chambersburg PA
CBHW071203090426
42736CB00012B/2430